To _____

From _____

My Favorite Recipe:

Signed _____

Date _____

First Edition
FOR ADDITIONAL COPIES, USE ORDER BLANKS IN
THE BACK OF THE BOOK OR WRITE DIRECTLY TO:
LaFray Publishing Company
P.O. Box 76400
St. Petersburg, Florida 33734   813-821-3233

Printed in the United States of America
International Standard Book Number: 0-942084-07-1
Library of Congress Card Catalog Number: 83-082687
First Printing: February 1984
0 9 8 7 6 5 4 3 2 1

PUBLISHER: Joyce S. LaFray-Young
TEXT BY: bj Altschul
PHOTOGRAPHY: bj Altschul
EDITORIAL FOOD CONSULTANTS:
Susan Shepard
Laura DeSalvo
Joyce LaFray-Young
COVER ART AND ILLUSTRATIONS BY: Adele Sgro
Pat Stockey
ASSISTANT TO THE PUBLISHER: Betty Jo Schies
TYPOGRAPHY AND DESIGN: Mariner Typographers Inc.
Additional photos courtesy of Florida State Archives,
Tallahassee

The following songs or excerpts thereof are printed with permission:
I Want To Be A Florida Cracker © 1977 Clifford J. Buckosh
Back Roads © 1982 Don Grooms
Mangrove Buccaneer © 1975 Dale Crider
Hold Back The Waters Of Lake Okeechobee © 1980 Will McLean
I'm A Cracker (Carl Allen's Song) © Frank Thomas

FAMOUS *florida!* ™

COVER ART BY ADELE SGRO

LaFray Publishing Company
St. Petersburg, Florida

I Want To Be
A Florida Cracker

Wish my mama knew how to cook swamp cabbage
Wish my daddy had a rattlesnake hide
Wish I knew how to fix some conch fritters
Wish I had me a Seminole bride.

Chorus:
  I want to be a Florida Cracker
  But I'll never get a chance to try
  I want to be a Florida Cracker
  But I'll be a damn Yankee 'til I die.

Love them alligator, pink flamingo
Kumquat, avocado, Key Lime pie
Can't get enough of that
Sunshine surf's up
Never get enough of that clear blue sky.

Osceola, Flagler, Ponce', Menendez
All knew that they found something good
Key West smugglers, Tarpon sponge divers
Never would leave even if they could.

To the people of Florida
—past, present and future—
and especially for
those who preserve the state's native foodways
in places where everyone may savor
these recipes

NOTES FROM THE TEST KITCHENS

For those of us in the test kitchens, testing the recipes for CRACKER COOKIN' was a unique experience. Some of the cooking procedures were new to us. Some of the ingredients were unusual. We had no idea that there were so many interesting ways to prepare swamp cabbage—we had seen it only in salads. The fried steak, much to our surprise, wasn't the least bit greasy. The quick frying sealed in the juices and the flavor. The Indian recipes proved to be delightful. We'd never tried an "Indian burger" before. And, we discovered that trying regional cooking methods can indeed expand one's culinary education.

Many of the recipes were submitted in bulk quantities that we had to alter for family-sized portions, because our aim was to make the recipes as easy as possible to follow. The ingredients are listed in the order of use. Where appropriate, we noted substitutions where an ingredient may be difficult to find in your area. Please note that cooking and preparation times are approximate, since everyone works at a different speed. There are also heating variations in gas and electric stoves.

Here are a few suggestions:

• Before marketing and planning your meal, read the recipe over carefully to eliminate any surprises. Several recipes have an overnight marinating time.

• Consult your local butcher for unusual cuts of meat called for so he can help you choose the best cuts or recommend alternatives.

• Don't be afraid to try a recipe that sounds unusual or uses ingredients in an unusual way. Most likely you will be pleased with the outcome.

• Welcome to this adventure in CRACKER COOKIN'. We know that you will enjoy it as much as we have!

Laura DeSalvo
Susan Shepard

A NOTE
FROM THE PUBLISHER

Here's your guide to THE OTHER FLORIDA, the real Florida, as we residents know it to be. You'll discover foods that Floridians have been proud of for many years, at remote restaurants that you might otherwise never know. CRACKER COOKIN' introduces you to the people, the scenery and the Florida back-country that has long been a secret to many. Author Marjorie Kinnan Rawlings called it an enchanted land, and indeed it is.

The eateries selected were carefully chosen and are much more than just restaurants. . .they're statements of Florida's heritage with much information about our past traditions in food preparation.

bj Altschul, our writer, has truly made this a labor of love. Her thirsty interest in THE OTHER FLORIDA, together with her enthusiastic devotion to our Sunshine State, have made this the story of Florida and one that we invite you to enjoy along with us. Just as Marjorie Kinnan Rawlings, author of *Cross Creek,* said about her homeland, we can also say about Florida, that she "belongs to the wind and the rain, to the sun and the seasons, to the cosmic secrecy of seed, and beyond all, to time."

Whether you enjoy these recipes in the restaurants or in the comfort of your home, we know that you'll enjoy your tour of Famous Florida!

ABOUT THE AUTHOR

Though not a Florida Cracker by birth or occupation, bj Altschul has lived in the Sunshine State long enough to consider herself a "semi-native." Through her activities as a founding member of the Florida Folklore Society and a volunteer at the annual Florida Folk Festival in White Springs, she has cultivated friendships with many talented individuals who *are* "Crackers," a "Cracker" being one who was born *and* raised here.

Professionally, her years of experience as a public relations counselor, editor and writer for city, regional and tourist publications have brought her in frequent contact with much of the state's history and its traditions. bj is a frequent contributor to local, state and national publications. At present, she is involved in her own consulting practice, Capital Communications of Tampa.

Listed in WHO'S WHO IN THE SOUTH AND SOUTHWEST, Ms. Altschul is an active member of the Public Relations Society of America, the Florida Freelance Writers Association, the Florida Motion Picture & Television Association, and the National Association of Creative Children and Adults. She has served as a grant review panelist for the Fine Arts Council of Florida and lecturer for the Florida Suncoast Writers' Conference.

Originally from Norfolk, Virginia, she now calls Tampa home. A Florida resident since 1967, she attended Goucher College in Towson, Maryland, and completed her Bachelor of Arts in Interdisciplinary Social Science as a Dean's List student at the University of South Florida. Currently she is working on her thesis for a Master of Arts in American Studies, a natural basis for compiling this engaging review of Cracker foodways in Florida. Her writing and organizational ability have been praised by Wernher von Braun, the Salvador Dali Foundation, Florida Secretary of State George Firestone, and many business, media and academic professionals.

ACKNOWLEDGMENTS

Sometimes you don't know where a fragment of folklore comes from, just that it's there. So it is with much of the history in these pages. It could be a tidbit from an anecdote told by one of the restaurant owners. Or it could be a fact gleaned from the volumes of published Florida history. Or it could be a phrase that just "happened," perhaps from someone we met but we can't recall who or when or where or even how.

So it's difficult to thank every individual by name who directly or indirectly helped us compile this collection of recipes or contributed to the narrative. There are a few whom I'd personally like to single out because they've so greatly influenced my love for Florida and consequently this research. First, Cousin Thelma Boltin, mistress of ceremonies for the Florida Folk Festival, instills in all who meet her a deep feeling for the Florida of old, the Florida of nature. A special thank you also to the folksingers and folklorists who have granted permission to print the words to their songs or have in other ways lent their support and encouragement—Cliff Buckosh, Don Grooms, Will McLean, Gamble Rogers, Dr. Patricia Waterman, Dale Crider, Frank Thomas, Seminole Tribal Chairman James Billie, and numerous others.

The staff of the Florida Folk Life Center at the Stephen Foster Memorial deserves special mention, as do those at the Florida State Archives, the Department of Natural Resources, the Game and Fresh Water Fish Commission, and the Florida Collection at the University of South Florida Library.

We'd also like to thank the food editors of magazines and newspapers across the state and the many others who suggested these great eateries. And, of course, our deepest gratitude goes to the restaurant owners themselves for taking their time to share their stories and their recipes. This collection would not exist without them.

bj Altschul

Coffee Cup
Dainty Del
Hopkins Boarding House
PENSACOLA

Mama Cole's Cafe
PANAMA CITY

Wakulla Springs Lodge
WAKULLA SPRINGS

★ TALLAHASSEE

Julia Mae's Town-Inn
CARRABELLE

Latam Restaurant
La Teresita
Mel's Hot Dogs
Silver Ring Cafe (Ybor City)
TAMPA

Doe-Al Country Cookin'
Ted Peters Famous Smoked Fish
SOUTH PASADENA

Johnson's
CEDAR KEY

Allen's Historical Cafe
AUBURNDALE

Paul's
TARPON SPRINGS

The Chattaway
Jack's Skyway
ST. PETERSBURG

The Crab Trap
PALMETTO

State Farmers Market Restaurant
FT. MYERS

Buttonwood Bar B-Q
SANIBEL

Gator Grill
MARCO ISLAND

Parson's
MAYPORT

Robert's Dock
LAKE CITY

Mama Lo's
The Primrose Inn
GAINESVILLE

The Yearling
CROSS CREEK

Buddy Freddys
PLANT CITY

Acapulco Cafe
ZOLFO SPRINGS

Flora and Ella's
LaBELLE

S. W. Cowboy's
O'Steen's
Vilano Seafood Shack
ST. AUGUSTINE

Hampton's
DAYTONA BEACH

The Old Spanish Sugar Mill
DeLEON SPRINGS

Oviedo Inn
OVIEDO

The Catfish Place
ST. CLOUD

Suncrest
MELBOURNE

Ye Tower Lunch
LANTANA

La Esquina de Tejas
Malaga
MIAMI

The Spiral
CORAL GABLES

Miccosukee Restaurant
TAMIAMI TRAIL

Mangrove Mama's
SUGAR LOAF KEY

Half Shell Raw Bar
Pepe's Cafe
KEY WEST

florida

INTRODUCTION

Florida's history represents a melange of events, personalities, and influences from different countries. Its regional "foodways," according to folklore, are the enduring ways of preparing native foods along with the customs for serving them. Even though there isn't any one dominant theme behind the overall statewide cuisine, each section of the state and each of several major foods has made a contribution that is an integral part of Florida's culinary identity.

We must take issue with Waverley Root's assessment of Florida food as "characterized by an overwhelming abundance of raw materials and a rather spectacular absence of good cooking." On the contrary, we've found that it's just a matter of knowing *where* to look and *what* to look for.

This collection of recipes from "down-home" restaurants throughout Florida represents an effort to locate the places that still serve traditional dishes—dishes that evolved from the days of exploration, pioneer settlement, ethnic heritage unique to Florida, and the "good ol' days" of just a few decades ago. You'll discover several uses of the term "Cracker"—defined as not only someone who was born and raised in the Sunshine State, but also a "Cracker cowboy," a cow hunter who cracked his whip as he rustled herds of cattle.

How did we select the eateries in CRACKER COOKIN'? Through a variety of research methods and recommendations from folks around the state. We contacted food writers and editors, food aficionados, and just plain went looking for 'em. It wasn't so easy to find exactly the kinds of places we wanted in every community!

Most of the recipes were previously unpublished. It was genuinely rewarding to have found such a generous spirit among the owners who shared with us these special traditions and their contemporary favorites.

If you plan to visit any of these restaurants, call ahead to find out hours and days open. The restaurant business is highly changeable, and while most that we've included have done things the same way for decades, you never know when a change may occur.

Also, state regulations regarding protected species of flora and fauna may vary from year to year, so we've included information in the Appendix so that you may contact the appropriate agencies directly.

CRACKER COOKIN' is organized geographically so that you may use it as a tour guide in each region of the state. In those communities where we've included more than one restaurant, they're presented in alphabetical order.

You'll find the Appendix a great help in your quest for great cuisine. The Festivals Calendar will help you plan your travels around a food theme that is tied in with history. The Reference List will direct you to additional information about Florida's native cuisine.

We know you'll enjoy your journey through the back roads of Florida, into the kitchens where "mom and pop" establishments are very much alive.

Garrison Keillor, host of the popular *Prairie Home Companion* show broadcast weekly on the American Public Radio Network, personifies the warmth of small-town America. In this collection we offer you *our* version of what you might call a *"Cracker* Home Companion," an invitation to dine in "The Other Florida."

TABLE OF CONTENTS

Restaurants—in geographic order

Coffee Cup

Pensacola

It's just a plain white building on the outside and has just a plain 1950s-style decor on the inside. But Pensacola's Coffee Cup is one local institution that's been packing its customers in since the day it opened in 1945. The food is wholesome, the service is friendly, prices are low, and the take-out service for homemade pies is as busy as the restaurant itself.

The process of serving guests at the Coffee Cup is such a hubbub all day long that you'd be mistaken to think there's a quieter time of day to mosey in or out at leisure. The tables are filled almost from the moment the restaurant opens until it's time to close, and there's often a line of customers waiting for seats or for carry-out orders.

This busy eatery is known for good home-style food, and especially for Nassau grits. These are an original adaptation of traditional Southern grits, with tomato sauce and other ingredients added. The restaurant staff butchers its own beef and makes its own chicken steaks and cutlets. Long-time chef Willie Laird uses no instant mixes and insists on cooking everything long enough for all the flavors to be at their best.

1

Owners Frederick and Earline Cleaveland and various members of their family have owned the Coffee Cup since the early 1970s. Willie and several of the other cooks and waitresses have been there almost from the beginning. And they're on a first-name basis with many of their regular customers. Some have been coming here so many years that you could almost set your clock by when they arrive. The restaurant is popular with politicians, too—one who enjoyed the hotcakes was former Florida Governor Reubin Askew. On another occasion, the Coffee Cup even sent him some batter directly to Tallahassee, the state capital.

If you sit at the counter for breakfast, pay close attention to the short-order cooks at the grill. They'll flip some of the fluffiest omelets around, never missing a beat. And take a look around you. The seats at the counter may remind you of an old soda fountain of the 1950s.

It's a good place to start the day in this Panhandle city with its thriving Naval Base and delightful restored historic areas.

Directions: The Coffee Cup is at 520 East Cervantes. From I-110 into downtown, exit at Cervantes Street. Turn left (east) and drive to the Coffee Cup.

*While you're here: Home of the world's largest **Naval Air Station** and the Navy's precision flying team, the Blue Angels, Pensacola is considered a choice stateside assignment among service personnel. The **Sea and Land Survival Exhibit** and the **Naval Aviation Museum** show the history of American aviation. The aircraft training carrier, the **USS Lexington**, is open to the public when she is in port.*

Coffee Cup
Pensacola

SPANISH OMELET

2 eggs
2 oz. vegetable shortening or butter
   Spanish Sauce (see recipe for Amberjack with
      Creole Sauce, page 4)

Beat eggs in blender. Melt shortening or butter in
skillet. Pour eggs into skillet. As eggs begin to set
around edge of skillet, lift edges of eggs with spatula
so that runny part on top goes to bottom for cooking.
Fold omelet over itself and slide onto heated plate.
Pour hot Spanish Sauce over omelet before serving.
For a Western omelet add a mixture of 3 tablespoons
each of bell pepper and onion and ½ cup ham, cut
up, to the eggs in the skillet. Fold omelet.

Serves: 1
Preparation: 5 minutes
Cooking: 5 minutes

*"The Spanish Sauce adds a spicy tang to this simple
omelet."*

AMBERJACK WITH SPANISH SAUCE

Make Spanish Sauce ahead:

SPANISH SAUCE
1   large onion, chopped
2   stalks celery, chopped
1   bell pepper, chopped
    bacon grease
1   small can crushed tomatoes
1   small can tomato sauce
1½ t. flour
1½ t. butter
2   bay leaves
    pinch sweet basil
    dash hot sauce
    dash Worcestershire
    dash Soy sauce
    salt and pepper to taste

Sauté onion, celery, and pepper in a little bacon
grease. Pour in tomatoes and tomato sauce and mix.
Make a roux* by melting the butter and stirring in the
flour. Cook for a minute or two, then add to tomato
mixture. Stir mixture until it thickens and comes to a
boil. Add bay leaves and remaining ingredients and
simmer for 10 minutes or until mixture reaches a
gravy base consistency. Stir frequently.

*See Glossary.

While sauce is cooking prepare fish:

6   fillets of fish, cut in 6-oz. pieces
¼   C. clarified butter
1   T. chopped parsley
2   t. lemon juice
    paprika

Pat fillets out flat with a pounder. Melt clarifed butter
and cook slowly until light brown. Stir in parsley and
lemon juice and simmer for about 5 minutes. Place
fillets in an oven-proof buttered pan and pour lemon
butter over. Sprinkle paprika on top. Pour warm
Spanish Sauce over the fish. Bake at 350°F. for
30 minutes until fish flakes. Check after 15 minutes.

Serves: 6
Preparation: 20 minutes
Cooking: 30 minutes

*"Amberjack is a Gulf fish, a member of the salmon
family. Try this tasty sauce with any other fat fish
such as pompano, sea trout or halibut. Excellent!"*

NASSAU GRITS

---

2   **C. Quaker quick grits (or your favorite brand)**
1   **onion, chopped**
1   **bell pepper, chopped**
4   **strips bacon**
1   **C. leftover ham or sausage**
1   **small can tomatoes**

Prepare grits according to instructions on package. Sauté onion and pepper. Fry bacon until crisp, saving grease. Add bacon and leftover ham or sausage to onions and peppers. Mix in tomatoes. Add entire mixture to grits, adding bacon fat to reach desired texture. Heat just enough to warm through. Stir well and serve.

Serves: 2–4
Preparation: 10–15 minutes
Cooking: 5 minutes

"This is an easy dish that tastes even better when reheated. Make your own variations with your choice of 'odds and ends' or leftovers. We didn't have any leftovers, so we made this as a side dish with pork chops. Enjoy it meal after meal!"

Coffee Cup
Pensacola

RUTABAGA CHUNKS

1 large rutabaga
2 oz. ham skin
water
dash sugar
salt and pepper to taste

Peel rutabaga, slice in quarters, and then cut in
chunks. Boil ham skin until tender, about an hour.
Add rutabaga chunks and enough water to cover.
Add a dash of sugar, salt, and pepper to taste. Cook
until tender, about 30 minutes on top of stove or 1
hour in oven, to allow the meat flavor to be absorbed
into the vegetable. An alternative way to prepare this
dish is with ham or bacon stock (including the
grease) instead of water and ham skin.

Serves: 10-12
Preparation: 1 hour
Cooking: 1½-2 hours

*"This is a good side dish with pork chops and
greens. Be sure to add the dash of sugar because it
really brings out the flavor."*

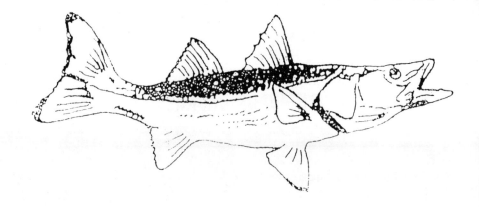

Dainty Del

Pensacola

Even though the Greek flag isn't one that gave Pensacola its claim as the "City of Five Flags," there has long been a very sizable Greek community here. During the first half of the 19th century the city elected the first Greek mayor in the United States. And from the early 1920s, the Dainty Del Restaurant has been Greek-owned and managed.

Today's owner, George Georgiades, and his three sons cater to a large and devoted following. Devotees used to come for the hamburgers, oysters, and sandwiches when they couldn't afford more expensive meals. Now that these "fans" are retired, they still come to the Dainty Del, which, as George says, has kept its image over the years. As the oldest seafood restaurant in town, it has remained popular with anniversary celebrants and many of the World War II Golden Eagle pilots in town. A retired county judge from Pensacola characterizes the restaurant as a place for the *real* old-timers, folks who can recount some of the city's most interesting and intricate historical details.

George will probably tell you a few details himself if he's out front hosting and not busy in the kitchen. He's the kind of host who likes to be everywhere at once, always making sure he's feeding his guests good food "just like *I* want to eat it. I was never satisfied for someone else to cook for me," he says of his days growing up, when he used to cook alongside his mother at home in Greece.

"There's something in every human being, every cook to create," he adds. For him the specialty is charcoal-broiled seafood to preserve the best fish flavor. He does most of the "important" cooking himself, all based on recipes and techniques that he learned from his mother.

One day he'll be testing a new kind of grill. The next day he'll be experimenting with rotisserie sticks in a new barbecue so that he can roast the best Greek chicken, lamb, pork and beef. With a twinkle in his eyes, he'll tell you what the day's specials are—Whole Broiled Snapper or Spanish Mackerel, Stuffed Whole Flounder, or Oysters Rockefeller. Do try the oysters; he insists on buying "the biggest and the best" for his customers.

Ask him why so many Greeks came to Pensacola and became involved in community life and fishing. He'll tell you it's because they love the water. It's a beautiful view here.

Directions: The Dainty Del is at 286 North Palafox Street. From I-110 into downtown, exit at Cervantes Street and turn right (west). Turn left (south) on Palafox Street to address; Dainty Del is on the east side of the street.

While you're here: Pensacola is a history-lover's delight. The town was actually the first attempt at settlement in the New World, predating St. Augustine by six years. But the Spanish colony organized by Don Tristan de Luna was abandoned when ships bearing supplies were wiped out by storms at sea. Today, the **Seville Square Historical District** *presents the Shopkeepers of Historic Seville. There are more than 30 shops, galleries, restaurants and museums in restored and well-maintained old cottages and mansions. There's probably not a single 19th–century wooden architectural style* **not** *represented. Special events throughout the year recreate everything from a Gay'90s atmosphere to the city's Spanish heritage during the* **Fiesta of Five Flags**, *every May.*

CHARCOAL-BROILED SHRIMP

---

6   **jumbo shrimp per serving**
½   **oz. butter (approximately)**
½   **oz. lemon juice (approximately)**
2   **pinches oregano**
2   **pinches salt and pepper**

Melt butter in small saucepan with an equal amount of lemon juice. Add oregano, salt and pepper. Coat shrimp in mixture and broil for 2 minutes on each side over hot coals.

Serves: 1
Preparation: 3 minutes
Cooking: 5 minutes

"A quick way to prepare this Florida specialty."

CHARCOAL-BROILED SCAMP

---

1   9-10 oz. scamp* steak per serving
2   oz. olive oil (approximately)
2   oz. lemon juice (approximately)
2   pinches oregano
2   pinches salt and pepper

Make a mixture of equal amounts of olive oil and
lemon juice. Add oregano, salt and pepper. Brush
mixture on scamp steaks and cook over hot coals.
Baste every few minutes. Scamp is done when juices
stop flowing.

Serves: 1
Preparation: 5 minutes
Cooking: 20-30 minutes

*"This is similar to Charcoal-Broiled Shrimp, but you
do need to cook the scamp longer. Scamp is a super-
tasting fish."*

*If not available, substitute any firm lean fish.

Dainty Del
Pensacola

CRAB MEAT DRESSING

---

1   C. mayonnaise
1   C. mustard
1   C. onions, chopped
1   C. celery, chopped
1   C. crushed crackers
        at least 2 lbs. *fresh* cooked crab meat
1½–2 T. fish or Old Bay seasoning
        salt and pepper to taste

Mix all ingredients well. Bake or broil until hot. Can be served stuffed in shrimp or alone, with some rice on the side. Alternative method: stuff shrimp and fry until shrimp are done.

Serves: 4–6
Preparation: 20 minutes
Cooking: 7–10 minutes

"This is an easy dish for lunch or dinner. Serve with a green salad."

BROILED SNAPPER OR MACKEREL

**6-8 oz. fresh snapper or mackerel fillets
fresh onion, chopped or sliced
pepper (no salt!)
pinch oregano
paprika
juice of half a fresh lemon
olive oil to taste
parsley, chopped, to garnish**

Place fillets in a buttered baking dish. Add onions.
Sprinkle very lightly with pepper, oregano, and
paprika. Add lemon juice and olive oil. Bake at 350°F.
until fish flakes, about 10 to 15 minutes. Garnish with
parsley and serve.

Serves: 1
Preparation: 10 minutes
Cooking: 10–15 minutes

*"A simple way to enhance the flavor of fresh fillets.
Serve with boiled new potatoes, buttered and
parsleyed, or serve with buttered wide noodles."*

SPECIAL SNAPPER

4   8-9 oz. snapper steaks
    olive oil
1   large onion, finely chopped
1   bell pepper, finely chopped
1   small carrot, finely chopped
4-5 large mushrooms, quartered
2-3 small fresh tomatoes, roughly chopped

Coat snapper with olive oil and broil in broiler or over hot coals for about 10 minutes or until done. Sauté all vegetables except tomatoes in about 2 tablespoons of olive oil. Spread sautéed vegetables and chopped tomatoes over snapper.

Serves: 4
Preparation: 5 minutes
Cooking: about 12-15 minutes

"Be sure not to cook the tomatoes. They make a pleasant contrast to the cooked vegetables."

Hopkins Boarding House

Pensacola

The setting and atmosphere at Hopkins Boarding House are reminiscent of a John Steinbeck novel—guests are all ages, transient and long-term residents, some weathered by experience and some just starting out their lives. In typical boarding house style, families and strangers sit together at the same table and no one remains a stranger for long.

"Would you pass the black-eyed peas and the spiced apples, please?"

"Sure. Where you from?"

And another friendly conversation begins.

Arkie Bell "Ma" Hopkins first entered the business in 1948 and did all the cooking herself. She emphasized the boarding house aspect, feeding only its three or four lodgers, with guests seated at a single long table. Now it's the other way around. The restaurant is the main part of the business, though there's still room for a half-dozen boarders at the present location on Spring Street. There are now three

15

dining areas, with a few family-size tables in addition to the long ones.

Ma Hopkins welcomes you into her home, which is located in the historic district of Pensacola. High ceilings, family memorabilia, antiques, and carved fireplaces lend a sense of nostalgia to the graceful old building.

What's different about boarding house dining is that you don't place an order from a menu. The food—and lots of it—is already on the table, and you just help yourself. At Hopkins Boarding House it's a Southern feast, everything from heaping bowls of grits at breakfast to an array of freshly cooked vegetables and fried chicken or an alternate entree at lunch and dinner. At one time, some of the vegetables were even grown in their own garden and picked fresh daily. This was no doubt a carryover from Ma Hopkins' having grown up on a farm. Today the vegetables are bought fresh from local farmers. At one time Ma Hopkins used to stay up all night baking pies by herself, but now that's a shared responsibility that extends to cobblers and puddings as well.

Another characteristic of a boarding house meal is that you can serve yourself as much as you like. Cheerful waitresses keep the large bowls filled all the time. Guests come and go throughout the meal. And when you're ready to leave, take your plate to the kitchen. You pay on your way out.

And with all the passing of food back and forth, a boarding house reach probably won't be necessary, but it's not out of place, either!

Directions: Hopkins Boarding House is at 900 North Spring Street. From I-110 all the way into town, turn right (west) on Cervantes Street (U.S. 90 and 98). Turn right again (north) on Spring Street to address.

*While you're here: Hopkins Boarding House is in the **North Hill Preservation District**, a 60-block area of restored homes from the late 19th and early 20th centuries, beautifully tree-shaded and a joy for a "Sunday drive." **Fort George Park** represents the only Revolutionary War battle fought in Florida, and **Lee Square** is a tribute to the Confederacy. Nearby downtown is peppered with historic churches, hotels, office buildings, and the **Saenger Theatre**, which was called "Florida's Greatest Showplace" when it first opened in 1925.*

MAMA'S FANCY RICE AND CHICKEN

1   **large (3½–4 lb.) fryer**
1   **C. rice, uncooked**
1   **medium onion, diced**
¾   **C. diced celery**
½   **C. diced bell pepper**
1   **small jar pimiento, diced**
    salt and pepper to taste

Cut fryer in quarters. Salt and pepper to taste. Bake in covered pan in 375°F. oven about one hour or until tender. Remove and cover to keep warm. Add three cups water to drippings and brown particles. Scrape all particles from pan. Place in saucepan with rice and vegetables. Cook until rice is done, about 45 minutes. Place in dish with chicken and serve at once.

Serves: 4
Preparation: 5 minutes
Cooking: 45 minutes plus one hour

"An easy main-course dish."

VERY GOOD FRUIT SALAD

(chill overnight)

1   lg. can pineapple tidbits
1   lg. can fruit cocktail
1   small jar maraschino cherries, halved
1   C. pecans, broken or coarsely chopped
1   8-oz. pkg. shredded coconut
1   small pkg. (10-oz.) small marshmallows
1   C. sour cream

Drain fruits well. Mix all ingredients and stir in sour cream. Refrigerate overnight before serving.

Serves: 8-10
Preparation: 5-10 minutes plus chilling overnight

"You can save the liquid from the fruits to use as a quick topping for ice cream. This recipe is perfect to take to a potluck supper. Or, halve the ingredients and serve to your family or guests."

LEMON CHIFFON PIE

---

1   C. boiling water
1   T. butter
2   large lemons
4   egg yolks
¾   C. sugar
3   T. cornstarch
10" baked pie crust

MERINGUE

4   egg whites
4   T. sugar
    pinch of cream of tartar

Place boiling water and butter in top of double boiler. Wash lemons. Grate rind and add to water and butter. Squeeze lemon juice into a cup. Beat egg yolks. Mix ¾ C. sugar and cornstarch with egg yolks, add lemon juice and beat well. Add this mixture to boiling water, butter and lemon rind. Cook and stir until thick. Beat egg whites, 4 T. sugar, and pinch of cream of tartar until stiff and fold half of this mixture into the lemon mixture, saving remainder for meringue. Pour into baked pie shell. Spread balance of egg whites on top and brown lightly in oven or under broiler. Keep a sharp eye on the meringue so it doesn't burn.

Serves: 8
Preparation: 20 minutes
Cooking: 15 minutes

"We tested this recipe early one morning. By noon it was all gone!"

Mama Cole's Café, Home of Soul Food, Panama City, Florida

Mama Cole's Café

Panama City

Some places that don't look like much from the outside belie the fact that inside is a soul that permeates every morsel of food served, down to the last crumb on the plate.

Such a place is Mama Cole's, home of soul food in Panama City for close to three decades. During that time, it seems, everyone in town has come to know Lucille Cole's sure hand in the kitchen. Located just a few blocks from Bay Memorial Hospital and downtown city office buildings, the tiny café has played host to countless private dinner parties, birthday celebrations, and other special occasions. Some folks who live in the region drive as far as 20 miles just for Mama Cole's home cookin'.

It doesn't matter that there are only five tables, decorated with red oilcloth tablecloths, or that the floor inside slopes to one side. The tangy aroma of barbecue sauce, ribs, chicken, cornbread, and turnip greens gets your olfactory senses in gear. It's the food and the hospitality that you remember most.

Daughter Mercy, who is grown now and a successful model and cosmetologist, used to stand on a chair and wash dishes when she was a child. Family members have helped run the café over the years, and today Mama Cole's nieces are the waitresses. Mama Cole herself first began cooking when she was 12, starting out in Enterprise, Alabama, her hometown. At the start of World War II she came to Panama City for what she *thought* was going to be a weekend vacation, but she never left. She married and a few years later opened the restaurant.

Mama Cole's routine is to shop early in the morning for the fresh food that will become the midday meal. She begins cooking by 8:30 a.m. Each day a separate menu is written out by hand for each of the five tables. Food is served piping hot for the lunch crowd and throughout the afternoon.

Mama Cole is usually so busy fixing the food that she can't leave the kitchen to greet all of her guests. But she solved the problem by placing a sign out front that reads, "Hello everyone. Thanks for stopping by. Have a nice day. God bless you, Mama Cole."

Now *that's* soul.

Directions: Mama Cole's Café is on the corner of Business 98 (6th Street) and Harmon Avenue. From scenic U.S. 98 coming from Tyndall Air Force Base, follow signs to Business 98. Stay on 98 to the intersection with Harmon, just a few blocks from the fire station. Or, coming from Panama City Beach and the U.S. Naval Reservation, follow U.S. 98 across the Hathaway Bridge and as far as Frankford Avenue. Turn right on Frankford, which deadends into Beach Drive, which is Business 98.

While you're here: Take your pick of resort facilities along the beach, or roam around the **St. Andrews State Recreation Area** *near Shell Island, where you'll find a restored turpentine still. There's also the* **Junior Museum of Bay County**, *which includes a re-created Pioneer Village farm from the late 1800s. Don't miss a longer drive along U.S. 98 through Fort Walton Beach and Destin, which many claim are the "world's most beautiful beaches." Sport diving and surfing are great here, too. The* **Miracle Strip Amusement Park** *offers 30 rides and attractions that will make you think of a year-round carnival midway.*

SMOTHERED PORK CHOPS

4-6 pork chops (allow 6-8 oz. per serving)
  salt and pepper to taste
  seasoning salt (or Accent)
  flour for dipping
  cooking oil

Season chops with salt, pepper, and seasoning salt.
Dip in flour and brown in cooking oil. Lower heat and
cook until pork chops are almost cooked through.

Serves: 4-6
Preparation: 3 minutes
Cooking: varies according to thickness of chops

for GRAVY:

2   C. water
1   onion, sliced
¼   C. flour for thickening (approximately)
     salt and pepper to taste
     seasoning salt to taste
     gravy coloring (such as Master Gravy, or your
       favorite brand)

Heat water in pan and add sliced onions. In separate
bowl, mix flour and seasonings and add to water with
whisk until mixture is desired thickness. Add gravy
coloring. Add cooked pork chops to gravy mixture
and simmer for 10 minutes.

Serves: 4-6
Preparation: 5-10 minutes
Cooking: 10 minutes

*"As Mama Cole makes it, the gravy is like a thick
breading that sticks to the chops. Pork chop-lovers,
this is it!"*

Julia Mae's Town-Inn, Carrabelle, Florida

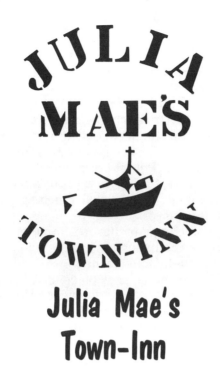

Julia Mae's Town-Inn

Carrabelle

A mere half-hour's drive from Apalachicola, oyster capital of Florida, there's a very little town famous as the home of the tiniest police station in the United States. The town is Carrabelle, on the shores of scenic route U.S. 98. The police station's headquarters are a telephone booth!

One thing that's *not* tiny in Carrabelle, though, is how much food you're served at Julia Mae's Town-Inn. For more than 30 years, Julia Mae Putnal has been making the most of seafood. A legend to the locals, she's the owner, manager, and chief cook at her popular roadside retreat. Each day's fresh catch is brought in by her husband, who's the chief angler. Her claim of "Serving the Finest Seafood in the South" is well deserved, and praise has even come from Florida's Governor, Bob Graham.

Nestled among tall pines, Julia Mae's is in a quiet, rustic setting. A treasure trove of shells and other findings from the region and its waters graces the walls. There's nothing fancy, mind you, but the ambiance is instantly inviting.

Oysters appear on the menu in at least a half-dozen sections. Any well-informed shucker can tell you that Apalachicola maintains more than 10,000 acres of oyster beds, producing some 90 percent of the state's entire crop. You can count on Julia Mae's to serve only the freshest.

The actual selection of seafood varies from day to day according to what Mr. Putnal brings in. You can be assured that there will always be more on your plate than you have room for. You'll just have to plan ahead so you can sample Julia Mae's famous pies. They're made fresh in her "pie house" and come in many flavors, from lemon meringue to Key Lime. Ask about her banana pudding, too. . . but be prepared for mountainous servings.

This is definitely not a fancy place for a festive dinner, but you'll feel right at home for a friendly, wholesome repast. As one customer wrote in the guest book, "It sure was great, Julia Mae. I'll be back Apalachicola!"

You'll say the same thing, too.

Directions: Julia Mae's Town-Inn is directly on U.S. 98 in Carrabelle, on the south side of the road. The town is on the Gulf of Mexico, about 50 miles south of Tallahassee.

While you're here: Besides its reputation for commercial fishing and oystering, Apalachicola has a history of being the third largest cotton-shipping port on the Gulf of Mexico during the 1830s. In that same period, Dr. John Gorrie invented the first mechanical ice machine, a predecessor of refrigeration and air-conditioning. The **Gorrie State Museum** *recalls the life of that era. If you're in town early in November, don't miss the* **Florida Seafood Festival**, *complete with fresh fish, a parade, arts and crafts, crab races, and oyster shucking contests.*

OYSTER STEW

12   oysters, shucked and liquor* reserved
1   C. milk
     salt and pepper to taste
1   t. butter

Place oysters in pot with liquor and cook until they shrink slightly. Add milk, butter, and seasonings and heat just until hot so that stew doesn't curdle. Serve with crackers.

Serves: 1
Preparation: allow 15 minutes shucking time per serving
Cooking: about 10 minutes

"This is a mild oyster stew. You may want to add Tabasco and/or Worcestershire sauce at the table."

*Liquor, that's the water inside the oyster.

JULIA MAE'S CHOCOLATE PIE

1	qt. chocolate milk
¼	lb. butter, melted
3	C. sugar
4	eggs, separated
5	T. cornstarch
	water to dissolve cornstarch
2	T. vanilla
2	9″ baked pie shells
½	C. sugar (for meringue)
	pinch of cream of tartar

Combine milk, butter and 3 C. of sugar and bring to a boil. Dissolve cornstarch in water and beat in with egg yolks. Add vanilla to cornstarch and egg mixture. Then add to milk mixture. Beat until thick. Cool. Pour into pie shells. To make meringue: beat egg whites with a pinch of cream of tartar and ½ cup of sugar. Continue beating until stiff. Heat in 400°F. oven until brown. Cool for 1 hour at room temperature before refrigerating.

Serves: 6 per pie
Preparation: 15 minutes plus 1 hour to cool
Cooking: 5–8 minutes

"For an even more chocolate flavor, add 1–2 tablespoons of chocolate syrup. Either way, this is a delicious pie for 'chocoholics.' "

Wakulla Springs Lodge

Wakulla Springs

In recent years dining in Tallahassee has become characterized by a number of very fine restaurants and chain establishments. There's little left in the independent middle. But less than a half-hour's ride south of town is a retreat from the city's three major industries—state government, Florida State University, and lobbying. The community of Wakulla Springs is a place where the country's pristine natural history seems sacred.

In a tranquil setting of virgin forest, Wakulla Springs visitors can ponder the constant flow of crystal clear water from the springs, formed from an underground river basin that pumps more than 600,000 gallons of water a minute. The spring name comes from a Creek Indian word for "mysteries of strange water." In prehistoric times, animals were trapped in caves that are now covered with water. Fossils of Mastodon bones and human clans have been found in the area.

Guests at the Lodge can enjoy the many talents of the late Ed Ball, financier and entrepreneur. The 4,000-acre Edward Ball Wildlife Sanctuary is a natural landmark registered with the Department of the Interior. The Wakulla Springs Lodge itself is an exquisitely designed piece of workmanship. Originally constructed as Ball's personal retreat, it has nonetheless always been open to the public. The ceiling in the lobby is painted with Indian and Spanish themes to commemorate the history of the site. Even though a sense of enduring elegance pervades the dining room, it isn't necessary for guests to dress formally. You're expected to stroll and revel in the outdoors, with informal attire appropriate at mealtime.

Chef Gernard Gowdy has applied the graciousness of Southern hospitality to the menu, and the setting is reminiscent of antebellum days. After the expected fried chicken, cornbread and grits, sample the Lodge's specialties—Navy Bean Soup, Shrimp Floridian (jumbo shrimp wrapped in bacon and served with Whole Broiled Tomatoes), Stuffed Cornish Hen, or tempting lemon and pecan pies. You'll notice a difference in the flavor of the coffee, attributed to the pure spring water so abundant here.

From the crystal water goblets and seasoning containers to the full-service place settings, you'll find all of the finishing touches common at far more expensive restaurants.

After dining, wander over to the gift shop with its 60-foot-long marble soda fountain, or return to the Wildlife Sanctuary. The restful environment is a treat. Enjoy.

Directions: Wakulla Springs Lodge is at the junction of SR 61 and SR 267. From Tallahassee, take U.S. 319 South to SR 61 South, turning east at SR 267. The entrance to the lodge is on the right.

While you're here: The **Jungle Boat Tours** *and the* **Glass-bottom Boat Tours** *offer marine insights you'll find practically nowhere else. Part of the show is the singing-storytelling recitation of the tour boat guides. It will remind you of the vocal impressions of spirituals and the blues. Watch for the legendary* **Henry, the Pole-Vaulting Fish** *while you take in some of the 154 species of birds that have been sighted here along with all manner of wildlife.*

GRILLED FROG LEGS

---

1   lb. fresh frog legs
    milk, water, or beer for soaking legs
3   eggs
1   qt. milk
    flour for dipping
    salt and granulated garlic to taste
    butter
    lemon wedges and fresh parsley, chopped,
       to garnish

Soak frog legs in milk, water, or beer for at least
2 hours. Season to taste with salt and granulated
garlic. Mix together eggs and milk and dip frog legs
in mixture. Roll in flour. Place on buttered grill or
griddle. Cook until brown on each side, about
10 minutes, turning once or twice using two large
spatulas. Garnish with lemon and chopped parsley.

Serves: 2
Preparation: 5 minutes plus 2 hours for soaking
Cooking: 10–15 minutes

*"Frog legs are all lean meat with no fatty tissue so
they're a good low-calorie dish. Chef Gowdy's trick is
to cover the legs with a pie tin while they're cooking
so they'll come out moist. Try them yourself and
you'll see why people rave about them!"*

SHRIMP FLORIDIAN

1   lb. medium shrimp (21-25 count), shelled and
       deveined
     about 8 strips of bacon, cut into 3 pieces each
       (1 slice bacon per 3 shrimp)
     paprika
     softened butter
     toothpicks

Wrap each shrimp in bacon and fasten with a
toothpick. Sprinkle lightly with paprika and dot with a
little butter. Broil in pan with a small amount of
water to prevent sticking. Turn once when bacon
begins to crisp. When cooked on both sides,
about 5 minutes, remove toothpicks and serve with
hushpuppies (see page 188) and whole broiled
tomatoes, below.

WHOLE BROILED TOMATOES

     one tomato per serving
     bread crumbs
     salt and pepper to taste
     butter
     Parmesan cheese

Remove stem from tomatoes and cut out pulp about
a third of the way in. Fill with bread crumbs and
seasonings to taste. Sprinkle with Parmesan cheese
and dot with butter. Place in a pan with a little water
to prevent sticking. Bake 15–20 minutes at 350°F.

Arrange shrimp around tomato. Serve garnished with lemon wedge and parsley if desired.

Serves: 3
Preparation: shrimp—5-10 minutes;
tomatoes—5 minutes
Cooking: shrimp—5-10 minutes;
tomatoes—15-20 minutes

"The tomatoes can be put under the broiler after baking just long enough to brown the cheese."

Mathews Bridge Barbecue, Jacksonville, Florida, March 1953 (Florida State Archives)

34

Parson's

Mayport

Parson's may best be described as a restaurant-museum. On its walls are mounted dozens of fish caught in local waters—bull dolphin, great white shark, yellowfin tuna, red bass, blue marlin, sailfish, snook, cownose ray, bulldozer, and black grouper, to name only a few. A light in the center of the dining room is made from four hammerhead sharks. Display cases of shells are nicely arranged near the entrance. Groups of school children often come on field trips, and it's common to see browsers taking pictures.

But the fish collection isn't all Parson's is known for. Friendly service and attention to each order are standard at this local institution. As you may guess, seafood is the specialty, everything from oysters and deviled crab to red bass and lobster. Snapper, trout, and flounder are the most popular dishes. The fresh seafood is brought in to be cleaned, filleted, and prepared on site.

Order your choice of fish either broiled or fried. Each dish is prepared individually. If you prefer to have a dish broiled, for example, but it doesn't appear that way on the menu, just ask. And do the same if you prefer your meal cooked without salt.

35

In addition to serving fresh seafood, Parson's makes its own Cheddar cheese dip, deliciously flavored with wine, a touch of garlic, and several "secret" ingredients. The restaurant also makes its own thousand island and bleu cheese salad dressings.

Many combination dinners are offered and are favorites among the locals. The most lavish combination is the Mayor's Special, originally created when Jacksonville Mayor Hans Tanzler hosted a dinner for other local dignitaries.. The special includes shrimp cocktail, oyster cocktail, more shrimp, more oysters, scallops, deviled crab, king crab, a half Florida stuffed lobster, hushpuppies, potato and salad. You'll not leave hungry.

Several military bases are a major part of Jacksonville's economy, and their personnel are frequent visitors at Parson's. The Mayport Naval Base is close by, and the restaurant draws many guests from Cecil Field and the Jacksonville Naval Base, both across the St. Johns River on the mainland. Celebrities performing at the nearby Alhambra Supper Club in Mayport are sometimes seen at Parson's, and movie actor George Hamilton became a "regular" while he was in town.

Much of the restaurant's success can be attributed to the owner's dedication. For Aubrey Parson, who purchased it in 1965, the restaurant is literally his life. He's there daily to do the cooking, year-round except for Thanksgiving and Christmas. His three sons manage the dining room on weekends and help with preparing the fine food.

It's certainly worth the ride for *this* fish story!

Directions: Parson's is at 4570 Ocean Street. From Jacksonville Beach, follow U.S. A1A north about six miles, towards the St. Johns River Ferry. About a half-mile before the ferry boarding area you will find the restaurant, on the north side of the street.

While You're Here: The **Fort Caroline National Monument** *is a reconstruction of the fort from which French adventurers attempted to establish a foothold in the New World in 1564. The* **Cummer Gallery of Art**, *in town, includes a wide span of European and American art, as well as Japanese Netsuke. The* **Jacksonville Zoo** *contains more than 700 species of animals, birds, and reptiles, and also features a miniature railroad ride.*

DREAM BOAT

3-4   oz. blue crab or king crab, cooked and picked
       over for shells and cartilage
3-4   oz. mushrooms, sliced (fresh or canned)
10-12 shrimp (30 count), boiled, shelled, and
       deveined
       dabs of butter
       wild rice, cooked (optional)

Place crab meat in a layer on bottom of casserole
baking dish. Add layer of mushrooms. Add layer of
shrimp. Spread with dabs of butter and heat in oven,
about 5 to 10 minutes at 300° to 350°F. If you wish,
add wild rice after the shrimp and then spread with
butter.

Serves: 1
Preparation: 5 minutes plus pre-cooking time for
             crab and shrimp
Cooking: 2-3 minutes in microwave; 5-10 minutes
          in conventional oven

*"Quantities may be adjusted according to appetite! A
simple but tasty dish."*

SEAFOOD AU GRATIN

3-4   **oz. red snapper (fillet), cooked**
10-12 **shrimp (30 count), boiled, shelled, and**
        deveined
3-4   **oz. blue crab or king crab, cooked and picked**
        over for shells and cartilage
        butter or margarine
        enough thick white sauce to cover (your
        favorite recipe)
2-3   **oz. cheddar cheese, sliced or in strips**
        paprika

Place red snapper in one end of oblong casserole dish. Place shrimp in middle and crab meat on other end. Spread with dabs of butter. For Au Gratin Sauce, first spread thick white sauce over top of seafood. Then add layer of Cheddar cheese. Sprinkle with paprika. Heat until warmed through, about 5 to 10 minutes at 300° to 350°F.

Serves: 1
Preparation: 5-10 minutes plus pre-cooking for
                  seafood and white sauce
Cooking: 5-10 minutes

"A seafood medley designed to make your taste buds sing!"

Apalachicola Harbor Day Festival, Franklin County, Florida, 1954 (Florida State Archives)

S. W. Cowboy's, St. Augustine, Florida

S.W. Cowboy's

St. Augustine

Perhaps the oldest seafood restaurant on St. Augustine Beach, S.W. Cowboy's was founded in 1963. It's always busy despite its out-of-the-way location, and with good reason. Servings are more than generous, lots of care goes into the preparation, and service is always with a smile, no matter how crowded the restaurant is.

Bill White "and company" bought the restaurant from the original owner, whose initials were S.W. and whose nickname was "Cowboy." The "and company" is five other partners, all of whom have been close friends for about 20 years. They searched for a business they could manage together and now their families *are* the staff.

These friends have done everything themselves, from renovating the building to writing out the menus on poster board mounted in inverted, heart-shaped straw fans. They've added a beautiful wood deck in the garden patio, a little fantasy café area where you can sip a drink while you wait for dinner. Germaniums abound, and the twinkly lights strung throughout the trees will make you think it's Christmas. Inside, the macramé canopies hand-crafted by the friends section off some of the booths for privacy, providing a nautical, East Indies flavor.

41

The lines that start to form an hour before Cowboy's opens attest to the restaurant's popularity, especially among locals and tourists who are wise enough to ask where the locals eat. Be prepared to wait ... but then, the garden makes it a pleasure.

Seafood is the specialty, both fried and broiled. It's always fresh as it's all caught locally. The oysters come served with a pair of gloves and a knife for you to shuck them yourself. They're piled up in a baking tin that's so enormous you're likely to offer some to the next table and find yourself striking up a conversation as a result. "Quickies," as they're called on the menu, are served without the extras that accompany the regular dinners. They're popular with those who have smaller appetites, but you really should leave room for dessert either way. The homemade pies are delicious. It's a joy to discover how easy these dishes are to prepare. One of the partners remarked that he hesitates to give out the recipes because no one will believe how simple they are!

Directions: S.W. Cowboy's is on Dondanville Road. From U.S. 1 North or South, take King Street (A1A South) to Anastasia Island. Stay on A1A South about eight miles from downtown St. Augustine, a half mile south of the Holiday Inn. Signs at Dondanville Road, on the west side of the street, direct you to the restaurant.

While you're here: Particularly if you're visiting during the summer you're in luck. A few miles north of Cowboy's on A1A is the **St. Augustine Amphitheatre**, *where the state play, the* **Cross and the Sword**, *is performed. It's a colorful musical pageant that re-enacts St. Augustine's founding in 1565 and was written by Pulitzer Prize-winning dramatist Paul Green.* **Marineland of Florida**, *with performing porpoises and a chance to hand-feed underwater creatures, is approximately 10 miles south of Cowboy's on A1A.*

S.W. Cowboy's
St. Augustine

COWBOY'S SPECIAL SHRIMP

(Allow 1 hour to marinate ahead)

1   pt. Kraft Catalina Dressing
¼   t. celery seed (optional)
1   C. lemon juice
1   t. liquid smoke
1   T. salt
3   cloves fresh garlic, chopped
1   lb. medium shrimp, peeled, deveined, split, with
        tails left on
     rice, cooked

Mix all ingredients together, except shrimp, to make dressing. Marinate shrimp in this mixture for an hour. Broil shrimp until tails stand up, about 3 minutes. Serve over rice.

Serves: 2-4
Preparation: 20 minutes plus 1 hour to marinate
Cooking: 3 minutes

"You'll sit up and take notice of this sauce. Add parsley for a garnish."

43

COWBOY'S BROILED SNAPPER

1   T. lemon juice
8   oz. red snapper fillet
1-2 T. butter or margarine, melted
    paprika
    tartar sauce
    lemons, sliced

Pour lemon juice and melted butter over fish. Broil for a few minutes on each side until tender and flaky. Sprinkle with paprika and broil 5 more seconds. Serve with tartar sauce and sliced lemons.

Serves: 1
Preparation: 5 minutes
Cooking: 6-10 minutes

"Simplicity's the secret, and the sauce complements the delicate flavor of the snapper."

S.W. Cowboy's
St. Augustine

COWBOY'S PINEAPPLE PIE

1 16-oz. tub (1 lb.) Cool Whip
1 14-oz. can condensed milk
1 20-oz. can crushed pineapple
½ C. pecans, chopped
2 T. lemon juice
2 9-inch graham cracker pie crusts

Drain pineapple. Mix ingredients and fill pie shells. Chill and serve.

Yields: 2 pies
Preparation: 5–10 minutes plus time to chill

"We filled one pie crust and froze the remaining mixture to use as an extra dessert. A delicious and surprising taste treat!"

O'Steen's

St. Augustine

It's been said that if good shrimp are to be had in St. Augustine, then O'Steen's will have them. Back when the Salvadore brothers discovered that night trawling would yield the sweet, jumbo pink variety now called St. Augustine shrimp, they practically changed the industry overnight. Competition for dock space became extremely cutthroat for a time, as shrimpers in the north around Jacksonville and in the south around Key West also developed night trawling techniques.

The restaurant's original owner, Bob O'Steen, had been a railroad man and had gone on strike with the Florida East Coast Railway when wealthy financier Ed Ball wouldn't give the workers a raise. Bob's folks had operated a restaurant during World War II, and he had peddled crab cakes on the street during the Depression. So, armed with recipes from his mother, he went into business for himself.

Meanwhile, Joanna, one of the daughters in the Salvadore family, married Lonnie Pomar, the present owner. Lonnie had started as a bus boy at O'Steen's when he was just a lad and, over the years, worked himself all the way to the top.

This modest business doesn't advertise in *any* tourist-oriented publications yet nevertheless serves a full house at every meal. As a testimonial to the owner's pledge to provide good food at good value, locals jest that when the prime lending rate goes up a point, the line outside gets four feet longer. Actually, the line outside is usually long. Reservations are taken at the window when you arrive. Or, if you don't want to fight the crowds, you can call in a carry-out order ahead of time.

The interior is cheery with a den-like feeling and fireplace. Paintings by local artists of beach scenes and pelicans decorate the walls. There are daily specials at super-low prices and special prices for children's servings. Ingredients are fresh, and from his years of experience, Lonnie can instantly tell whether the catch is recent. Frequently changing the cooking oil is the secret to the good color on the shrimp. The breading is light, a nice change from the "heavy" shrimp served elsewhere.

There's a choice of cocktail sauces for your seafood: the mild sauce, which is pink as a result of adding mayonnaise, or the hot sauce. When your waitress tells you it's hot, don't forget what she says. . . hot is *hot!* But hot sauce and datil peppers (a regional favorite found only in St. George County) go hand in hand in St. Augustine, and this is one of the best places to enjoy them.

Directions: *O'Steen's is located at 205 Anastasia Boulevard. From U.S. 1 North or South, turn east on King Street (A1A South), through downtown and across the Bridge of Lions. The road is now called Anastasia Boulevard, which you simply follow to the restaurant, on the south side of the street. The reservations and take-out window is on the side of the restaurant.*

While you're here: *After you've toured historic St. Augustine, enjoy the miles of wide, hard-packed sand beaches on Anastasia Island and at the* **Anastasia State Park***, which offers a variety of outdoor recreation. Coquina quarries on the island have provided shellrock for construction since 1600; many such structures still stand in the restored area. This is an ideal destination for walkers and bicyclists!*

DEVILED CRABS

---

1   lb. blue crab claw meat
1   small onion, diced
1   small bell pepper, diced
2   stalks celery, diced
4   regular hamburger rolls, ground into crumbs
¾   t. salt
1   t. pepper
1   t. thyme
2   large datil peppers*, ground (or any other hot
      pepper)
    oil for frying

Pick over crab carefully to remove any shell or
cartilage. Set aside. Combine all other ingredients
except oil. Gently fold in crab meat. Pat into cakes
about 2½ inches in diameter. Heat oil to 400°F. and
carefully slip cakes in. Deep fry for three or four
minutes. Drain and serve immediately.

Yields: 12 patties, about 2½ inches in diameter
Preparation: 10–15 minutes
Cooking: 3–4 minutes per batch

*"These spicy crab cakes are perfect served with a
red cocktail sauce or chili sauce. You can double the
recipe for a crowd or make smaller cakes for finger
hors d'oeuvres."*

*See Appendix: Florida Foods (Minorcan Specialties).

O'Steen's
St. Augustine

SUPER SHRIMP SAUCE

1   C. mayonnaise
¾   C. catsup
1   oz. Worcestershire
1   oz. horseradish
½   oz. A.B. hot sauce

Mix thoroughly and serve.

Preparation: 5 minutes
Yields: 2 cups

"This is light in color because of the mayonnaise, but don't be deceived—it's VERY tangy!"

—NOTES—

Vilano Seafood Shack

St. Augustine

The Vilano Seafood Shack is no exception to the prevalent use of datil peppers in recipes at St. Augustine's restaurants. The emphasis is on seafood, and what the datil pepper does for the Shack's clam chowder, crab meat stuffed mushrooms, and crab meat stuffing will turn first-timers into true believers. The combination of the seasonings along with the freshest of fresh shellfish is the "secret."

The Shack's owners, Nathan and Cynthia Vestal, have taken their cottage-like building, that was originally constructed as a service station in the 1920s, and converted it into an informal eatery. Its location is a quiet beach setting, great for enjoying cool ocean breezes. The relatively untouched serenity of Vilano Beach makes the Seafood Shack's location a prize that one doesn't want to see changed. Picnic tables and beamed ceilings reflect the casual atmosphere of the community.

Cindy Vestal has worked closely with outstanding chefs at such well-known resorts as Innisbrook, in Tarpon Springs. Nathan's expertise comes from years of experience with French chefs, and he personally chooses the best fish from the docks between Mayport (near Jacksonville) and Ponce

Inlet (by Daytona Beach). His specialty is sautéing and broiling, although lightly battered, deep-fried seafood is also available. You'll notice the difference in taste that truly fresh seafood has after you've sampled what some restaurants offer and call fresh.

One of the most pleasant aspects of a meal at the Vilano Seafood Shack is the personal attention from Cindy and Nathan. They enjoy chatting with guests, making them feel right at home. On Sundays it's typical for families to stay on the beach until mid-afternoon; then they amble into the Shack for champagne and delicious food. There's a special children's menu, too.

Seasonal items are offered when they are available, including Cedar Key stone crab claws, blue crab, and local clams that are steamed. If you don't see a particular kind of preparation you like on the menu, just ask. If all the ingredients are on hand, you can have your dish fixed any way you like.

And while you're dining, take time to look at the paintings and photographs by local singers Bob and Jolene Patterson, and other local artists. As you'll read on the menu, these seascapes are a reminder to us to "preserve what mankind did not create."

Directions: *The Vilano Seafood Shack is at 111 Vilano Road. From U.S. 1 North or South, take A1A North to Vilano Beach, a half mile east of the Vilano Beach Bridge. Where A1A makes a 90-degree turn north, look for the Seafood Shack, which is right at the corner.*

While you're here: *Do see the old town of St. Augustine. It's the oldest* permanent *settlement in the United States (Pensacola's the oldest* original *settlement), much of which has been restored so authentically that no cars are allowed on certain streets. After you've visited* **San Agustin Antiguo** *with its colonial period shops and craft demonstrations, see the huge* **Castillo de San Marcos** *fortress and the jail. Don't miss the ornate buildings created by Henry Flagler, the wealthy developer of the late 1800s: the* **Lightner Museum** *and* **Flagler College** *are both housed in buildings that used to be extravagant hotels Flagler conceived. They're monumental classics of American Renaissance architectural styles.*

THE SHACK'S SHRIMP AND SCALLOP SAUTÉ

1	oz. butter
¼	small onion, finely chopped
1	clove garlic, finely chopped
8-10	scallops
	approximately 6 mushrooms, sliced
8	shrimp, peeled, deveined, and butterflied
1	oz. Tamari sauce*
	juice of ½ lemon
	dash white pepper
	chopped parsley
	brown rice, cooked

Sauté first four ingredients until scallops are partially done. Add shrimp, Tamari sauce, lemon juice and pepper. Sauté a little longer until shrimp are done. Sprinkle chopped parsley over top for color. Serve over brown rice.

Serves: 2
Preparation: 5 minutes
Cooking: 5-7 minutes

"For variation, add fresh cauliflower or broccoli flowerettes before adding shrimp."

*Available in health food stores

BROCCOLI CRÊPES

---

12 crêpes*
2 heads broccoli
1 small onion, diced
4 T. butter
3 T. flour
2 C. milk
3 cloves garlic, minced
   salt and pepper to taste
6 oz. Swiss cheese, shredded

Make your favorite recipe for 12 crêpes and set aside. Steam fresh broccoli and chop flowerettes with some of the stems. Sauté onions in butter. Add flour and stir for a minute or two. Slowly add milk, stirring constantly. When mixture is thick, add broccoli, garlic, salt and pepper. Cook approximately 5 minutes, stirring constantly. Roll crêpes with filling. Place in a buttered, oven-proof dish or pan. Sprinkle with Swiss cheese. Bake for about 5 minutes at 350°F. or just long enough to warm throughout and to melt cheese.

Serves: 4-6
Preparation: 15 minutes (plus time to make crêpes)
Cooking: 15 minutes

"This is a delicately seasoned dish. What a way to present broccoli! You can make it ahead, refrigerate, and pop in the oven just before serving. Your guests will rave!"

*See glossary

Robert's Dock

Lake City

It would be natural to expect towns located near the intersection of two major interstate highways to be bustling metropolises or suburbs of some large cities. Instead, Lake City and the other communities near the junction of I-75 and I-10 are genteel reminders of an "undiscovered" Florida. They're the heart of Suwannee River Country, popularized in the songs of Stephen Foster.

Amid peaceful rivers where there is ample opportunity for quiet fishing, there is still growth. There are small town community and recreational facilities, Jaycees activities, and a surprisingly busy little airport.

Just across from the airport is one of the hallmarks of the region's home-style restaurants, Robert's Dock. Owners Robert and Emmie Chasteen have brought their whole family into the act. Many of the recipes came from Robert's mother, whose pineapple coconut cake was a hit in a local baking contest. All of the salad dressings are homemade, too. Both Robert's mother and grandmother had always been good cooks, and Robert had long dreamed of owning a restaurant while he was an interior decorator. When the chance to purchase what used to be Dave's Oyster Bar came along, Robert jumped and attractively remodeled the building. Today *North Florida Living* calls his restaurant one of the "top 10" in that part of the state.

A native of Lake City, Robert is a natural for serving good Southern cooking, especially after living in the country all his life. His original idea was to have a steak house. But he observed that more people here seem to prefer seafood when they dine out because they think it can be time-consuming to prepare at home. Hence, the menu reflects both Southern dishes and seafood, all artfully prepared. His secret for vegetables, he says, is to add a speck of sugar in each recipe to cut down the acid flavor.

Robert's young daughter is only one of the faces around this restaurant well-known to regulars. CBS sportscaster and Super Bowl announcer Pat Summerall calls Lake City home and is a frequent patron. The restaurant is a favorite with scuba divers exploring the nearby Ichetucknee and other fresh-water springs.

The vote for best dish on the menu is Robert's Seafood Casserole, served at dinner only, because it takes so long to prepare. It features shrimp, crab meat, and scallops in a thick, creamy base . . . delicious!

Directions: From I-75 take U.S. 90 east through town, about three miles out. Robert's Dock is on the north side of the road, across from the airport. Or, from I-10, take either U.S. 41 or 441 into town, and turn east on U.S. 90, as above.

While you're here: There's plenty to do in the Suwannee River Valley. There's the **Stephen Foster Memorial** *at White Springs, tubing down the clear* **Ichetucknee River,** *and the* **Battle of Olustee Festival** *each February. This festival presents a re-enactment of the largest Civil War battle fought on Florida soil, one of the South's largest victories.* **Florida Bicycle Tours** *originate here and head through the best of the state's back roads and foothills. They offer guided weekend and week-long trips, year-round, for every level of experience. Trips include visits to country lodgings, garden clubs, historical societies, and sometimes the homes of folk-singers, cloggers, and storytellers. Write to P.O. Drawer P, White Springs, FL 32096, for schedule information. Tell 'em we sent ya!*

Robert's Dock
Lake City

ROBERT'S SEAFOOD CASSEROLE

½   lb. cooked shrimp, peeled and deveined
½   lb. cooked crab meat, picked over for shells and
        cartilage
½   lb. cooked scallops
1   can cream of mushroom soup
1   can cream of celery soup
4   hard-boiled eggs, diced
¼   C. diced pimiento
¼   C. white wine, semi-sweet
2   T. Worcestershire
1   large bell pepper ⎫
1   large onion   ⎬ chopped, sautéed in butter
6   celery stalks   ⎭ until onion is translucent
        Seasoned Salt and pepper to taste
6   C. cooked rice
¾   C. mayonnaise
1   box Ritz Crackers, crushed
        melted butter

Mix all seafood together. Add soups, eggs, pimiento, wine, and Worcestershire sauce. Stir in sauteed onion, pepper, and celery. Add Seasoned Salt and pepper to taste. Add cooked rice. Blend in mayonnaise. Add enough Ritz Cracker crumbs to make mixture the consistency of cornbread dressing. Bake in a buttered casserole dish at 375°F. for 30 minutes or until it begins to bubble.

Top with rest of cracker crumbs. Drizzle with melted butter and cook until brown.

Serves: approximately 12
Preparation: 20 minutes
Cooking: 30–40 minutes

"This is a delicious casserole for a crowd; however, you can cut the recipe in half with excellent results. It's a specialty at Robert's Dock and can be yours, too!"

—NOTES—

MOM'S CHICKEN AND DUMPLINGS

1   large fryer chicken, cut up
2   qts. water
1   onion, diced
6   stalks of celery, diced
    salt and pepper to taste

Place chicken and rest of ingredients in a large pot. Add enough water to cover, about 2 quarts. Bring to a boil. Skim white residue off top. Lower heat and boil gently until tender, about 40 minutes. Skim residue from time to time. Remove chicken from broth and cool. Remove chicken from bones and cut up in bitesize pieces. Taste broth for seasonings and adjust if necessary. Add chicken back to broth. Bring broth to boil and add dumplings:

DUMPLINGS

3   C. plain flour
½   t. salt
1   heaping T. Crisco or other shortening
1   C. water
    milk

Sift flour and salt together. Add shortening and mix well. Add water and mix until dough is elastic and smooth. Divide dough and roll on floured board until thin. Rub flour across top and cut in oblong strips. Add to boiling broth and boil 5 minutes.

Add boned chicken and milk, if necessary, to bring it
to desired consistency. Mixture will thicken as it sits.

Serves: 4–6
Preparation: chicken—10 minutes;
   dumplings—15 minutes
Cooking: chicken—30–45 minutes;
   dumplings—5 minutes

*"As you can see, dumplings come in different shapes
and sizes! This is a delicious down-home, stick-to-
your-ribs meal in a pot. Leaving the chopped
vegetables in the broth adds extra flavor, but you can
remove them to serve on the side. You can do this
recipe in steps, cooking the chicken the day before
and making the dumplings just before you are ready
to serve."*

HONEY FRENCH DRESSING (SWEET AND SOUR)

½   C. tomato catsup
⅓   C. vinegar
⅓   C. honey
     dash Worcestershire
     pinch ground cloves
3   T. finely grated onions
     pinch salt
1   C. salad oil

Place all ingredients except oil in a mixing bowl or food processor. Mix together and beat well. Add oil slowly, drop by drop, beating constantly. Beat until dressing is thick and creamy. Store in a covered jar in refrigerator.

Yields: 2 cups
Preparation: 10 minutes

"This dressing is good, not only for your tossed salads, but it also goes wonderfully well on chicken. Marinate the chicken in the dressing for an hour; then bake in the marinade—tangy and tantalizing!"

Mama Lo's

Gainesville

One of the first places locals invariably mention when asked where to go in Gainesville for down-home cookin' at a good price is Mama Lo's. It's definitely an institution among students and soul and Southern food lovers.

Mama Lo is Lorine Alexander, whose mother and grandmother also fed these Gainesville people over the years. Though the restaurant seats only 35, Mama Lo serves 200 or more guests at every meal. Somehow, she manages to organize the preparation of about 15 entrees, 15 or 20 vegetables, side dishes, and homemade pies and cakes—all in a kitchen no larger than a typical home kitchen.

Not only are the choices varied, but you're given gigantic servings for very low prices. You'll not go away hungry after devouring stuffed peppers, chitlins (pig's insides, far more tasty than the name sounds), smoked sausage and yams, collard greens, blackeyed peas, and on and on.

Mama Lo decides on each day's selection early in the morning. She writes menus out in longhand for each of the eight tables. The rest of the day she spends cooking, her way of life for more than 17 years.

Most of the students who frequent her restaurant are from the University of Florida. Their official mascot is the alligator, and the region's nickname, appropriately, is "Gator Country." This is because 'gators are commonly attracted to sinkholes, often found in the area and formed when land collapses and fills with rain-water. Between the reptiles and the sinkholes, the students have plenty to poke fun at, but one thing's for certain—they're avid fans of Mama Lo's cooking.

You will be, too.

Directions: Mama Lo's is at 618 NW 6th Street. Take SR 24 (Archer Road) east from I-75. SR 24 merges into U.S. 441 (13th Street). Stay on 441 past the University of Florida campus (on the left) and turn east on NW 5th Avenue. Then turn north on NW 6th Street to address. Mama Lo's is on the west side of the street, across from the police station.

While you're here: One of the major sinkholes that provides insight into geologic formations is the **Devil's Millhopper** *site, just north of town on SR 232. It's popular for cave diving and nature trail hiking. Or you can arrange for a guided ranger walk. Eleven miles south on U.S. 441 is the 18,000-acre* **Paynes Prairie State Preserve**, *a fresh-water marsh with guided walks. The Preserve was named for the Seminole chief who fought for the property some 200 years after the Timucuan chief Vitachuco died defending it against the Spaniards.*

CHICKEN AND RICE

---

2   small frying chickens, cut into serving pieces
1½   qts. water
1   bell pepper, chopped
1   stalk celery (including leaves), chopped
1   medium onion, chopped
4   cubes chicken bouillon
     salt and pepper to taste
2   lbs. raw rice (Uncle Ben's or your favorite brand)
     yellow food coloring (optional)

Combine all ingredients except rice and food coloring
in a large pot. Cook, covered, over medium heat for
35 minutes. Add rice and an additional quart of water.
Cover and simmer another 25 minutes. Add food
coloring if desired and taste for seasonings.

Serves: 10–15
Preparation: 15 minutes
Cooking: 50 minutes

*"This is a simple but tasty dish. It is easy to cut the
amount of ingredients to make a family-sized dish."*

Mama Lo's
Gainesville

STRING BEANS

---

3 16-oz. cans string beans, drained
1 qt. water
1 small onion, diced
10 small white potatoes, diced
1 T. butter
   salt and pepper to taste

Drain juice from cans of string beans. Place all ingredients in large pot and cook until onions and potatoes are tender, about 15 to 20 minutes.

Serves: 8–10
Preparation: 5–10 minutes
Cooking: 15–20 minutes

"A quick side dish."

OLD-FASHIONED SWEET POTATOES

---

4   large sweet potatoes, cooked, peeled, and sliced,
     or a 1-lb. can of sweet potatoes, drained and
     sliced
2   C. sugar
3   C. water
1   T. vanilla
     pinch nutmeg
½   T. lemon juice
1   T. butter

Lay out sweet potato slices in a buttered baking dish
or pan. Mix remaining ingredients, except butter, and
pour over potatoes. Dot with butter. Place in oven and
bake for 35 minutes at 350°F.

Serves: 6-8
Preparation: 10 minutes
Cooking: 35 minutes

*"The potatoes will have an intriguing sweet taste but
will not be candied."*

Mama Lo's
Gainesville

HOPPINGJOHN

---

1 lb. blackeyed peas
3-4 thick slices salt pork
6 C. water
1 lb. Uncle Ben's rice
   salt and pepper to taste
1 T. butter
   pinch sugar .

Mix blackeyed peas and salt pork in water and boil gently for 30 minutes. Add remaining ingredients and simmer for 35 minutes longer. Add additional water as needed, stir often.

Serves: 6
Preparation: 30 minutes
Cooking: 35 minutes

"This is a classic and very traditional soul food dish."

GARDEN SALAD

1 head lettuce, broken into small pieces by hand
1 cucumber, thinly sliced
½ bell pepper, thinly sliced
1 carrot, thinly sliced
2 tomatoes, thinly sliced
½ stalk celery, chopped

Toss all ingredients. Serve with homemade dressing below.

MAMA LO'S HOMEMADE DRESSING

½ C. mayonnaise
1 T. vinegar
1 T. sugar
1 T. Worcestershire
½ C. tomato catsup
½ t. garlic powder
salt to taste

Mix all ingredients and stir well. Chill.

Serves: 6-8
Preparation: 10 minutes plus time to chill

"This is nearly a meal in itself. The dressing is reminiscent of a Louis dressing (for crab or shrimp Louis salad). Serve with a hot or cold soup and French bread or bread sticks."

The Primrose Inn, Gainesville, Florida

The Primrose Inn

Gainesville

Thomas Wolfe, writing in *You Can't Go Home Again*, says, "Some things will never change. Some things will always be the same. Lean down your ear upon the earth, and listen."

So it seems with The Primrose Inn, founded by Mrs. Byron Winn, Sr., in 1924, later owned by her son, Byron Winn, Jr. (a University of Florida graduate and mayor of Gainesville in 1963), and now owned by John McCraw. John, or Jack, as the regulars call him, didn't want to change a good thing when he bought the restaurant in the mid-1970s. Chef Boston Cobb and several others of the original staff are still at the Inn today. The menu still lives up to its reputation for tasty home-style food at reasonable prices, and the exterior blend of stick style and stone architecture is the same though the interior has been renovated and enlarged several times.

Just ask "Cousin" Thelma Boltin. The white-haired *grande dame* of the Florida Folk Festival has been a several-times-a-week customer for years and years. It's a favorite also with "Florida's Troubadour," Gamble Rogers. If you catch either of them there, you may be treated to an earful of memorable tales and folklore about the state!

Now Jack McCraw, though he hails from Alabama and the University of Tennessee, has found that many old University of Florida grads still remember The Primrose Inn. The yeast rolls were a big hit in the old days, and they still are, to the tune of some 1,500 a day. They used to be served with syrup and honey, but then there wouldn't be many of the great desserts sold. "My mother used to make 'em," says Jack. "We still punch them out of the dough by hand."

Daily specials and typed inserts on the menu offer a full range of Florida and Southern home cooking. There's everything from catfish and mullet to scalloped eggplant, cheese grits, and salmon croquettes. And because the building itself was once used for accommodations as well as meals, it still has the cozy feeling of home, from the fireplace in the lobby to the large, L-shaped dining area.

When Mrs. Winn first established the restaurant, it was popular to use names of flowers and trees for new businesses. In the years since, The Primrose Inn has become a Gainesville institution.

Directions: The Primrose Inn is at 214 West University Avenue (SR 26). From I-75 north or south, take the SR 26 exit east past the university campus, all the way into downtown to address. Or, from U.S. 441 north or south, turn east on University Avenue to address.

While you're here: Gainesville's main "industry" is the **University of Florida***, the state's oldest. It's a challenge not to get lost among the original and the new buildings. Don't miss the* **Florida State Museum***, among the top 10 natural history museums in the country and the top in the South. The* **University Art Gallery** *is also noteworthy. Or just drive leisurely around some of the residential neighborhoods, which are gracefully shaded by lush green oaks on gently rolling terrain.*

SCALLOPED EGGPLANT

1   eggplant, peeled and diced
½   stick margarine or butter
½   gallon milk
5   eggs
½   green pepper, chopped
1   t. chopped pimiento
1   medium onion, chopped
1   C. bread crumbs
1   C. crushed saltine crackers
1   4-6 oz. can Parmesan cheese
    salt and pepper to taste
    grated sharp or mild Cheddar cheese.

Boil eggplant until just tender. Drain and mash. Add margarine. Set aside. Combine eggs and milk with the remaining ingredients (except Cheddar cheese) and mix well. Pour mixture into a buttered baking dish. Spread evenly and sprinkle with grated Cheddar cheese. Bake in 350°F. oven for 30 minutes or until brown on top. It will have the texture of a souffle.

Serves: 4-6
Preparation: 15-20 minutes
Cooking: 30 minutes

"This goes well with broiled steak and sliced tomatoes."

The Primrose Inn
Gainesville

CORNBREAD DRESSING

1   pan cornbread (your favorite recipe), crumbled
½   as much bread, crumbled
2   T. chicken base or bouillon
½   small onion, chopped
1   stick celery, chopped
     sage, to taste
2   eggs, slightly beaten
¼   stick margarine or butter
     paprika

Mix cornbread and bread together using a fork.
Combine chicken base, onion, and celery, and stir
into bread mixture. Sprinkle lightly with sage. Stir in
eggs. Add mixture to a greased baking pan and
spread evenly. Dot with margarine or butter and
sprinkle with paprika. Bake 15–20 minutes in a
350°F. oven.

Serves: 5
Preparation: 15 minutes
Cooking: 15–20 minutes

*"This is a winner as an accompaniment to pork or
chicken. Or, stuff your turkey with it and it will
indeed be 'gobbled'!"*

The Yearling

Cross Creek

The traditional flavors of Florida, as recorded by Pulitzer Prize-winning author Marjorie Kinnan Rawlings, are kept alive at The Yearling. Although the restaurant is slightly fancier and a little higher priced than most of the others in our collection, its roots are as Cracker Florida as you can find.

Cross Creek is typical of the kind of small town that used to be prevalent all over the state. Sure, there are still many fishing villages and quiet communities, but we tend to forget about them in the sweep of "progress" along the coastline and its burgeoning population centers. Meanwhile, at The Yearling, owners Pat and Herb Herman have played host to everyone from the late Mrs. Rawlings' husband to locals and patrons from the furthest corners of the state.

Back in the 1930s, the period about which Mrs. Rawlings wrote so much, her neighbor Boss Brice used to host outdoorsmen who came to hunt, fish, and enjoy their catch. It's much the same today with the Hermans. There are seven cozy little cabins where guests can stay. Mrs. Herman tells about some Japanese visitors who came for a weekend and became so fascinated with the stories told by one of the teenagers who grew up around Mrs. Rawlings that they stayed three weeks!

The Hermans' interest in food and agriculture goes back to their 27 years in the poultry business in North Florida. Now retired from that endeavor, they take great pleasure in introducing newcomers to native foods served in a gracious environment. The "Cross Creek Special" is a tasty selection of catfish, frog legs, and cooter, all lightly breaded and fried. Cooter is what the natives call the soft-shelled turtle, a delicacy about which Mrs. Rawlings was particularly enthusiastic. It's an education to read how Mrs. Rawlings and her Cross Creek neighbors obtained and prepared the ingredients at hand in the woods. But of course, the Hermans do have the advantage of easier methods of preparation. Adjacent to the restaurant, The Yearling's gift shop has all of Mrs. Rawlings' books, including *Cross Creek Cookery*, as well as other souvenirs. Many of the original Cross Creek recipes read just like short stories.

Life in these parts has been immortalized on film in the 1983 production of *Cross Creek* by Robert Radnitz Productions in Culver City, California. Folks at The Yearling and in town were thrilled to entertain the cast and the crew during the filming. The Yearling is a fine location both to savor Cracker food and to enjoy the outdoors and the Hermans.

Directions: Driving from Gainesville, take I-75 south to SR 20. Turn south (right) where 20 intersects with Route 325, by the Lochloosa Wildlife Management Area. It's about eight miles on 325 to The Yearling, which is on your right.

While you're here: The **Marjorie Kinnan Rawlings State Historical Site** *is the author's restored Cracker home. Notice how the kitchen is set off by a breezeway. This prevents cooking heat from raising the temperature in the rest of the house. Cross Creek's location between Lochloosa and Orange Lakes is great for fishing, especially for bass, speckled perch, and bream.*

CROSS CREEK SPECIAL

catfish, cleaned (scrape out silky black inside
   from stomach with a spoon)
frog legs (buy already skinned and cut off feet)
cooter (buy in 1 to 3-lb. pieces and cut into
   portions like chicken)
self-rising flour, or cornmeal for dipping
milk
cooking oil

Keep cooter or frog legs covered with ice cubes from
1 to 4 hours in refrigerator until ready to use. This
tenderizes the meat and takes away some of the
gamey flavor. (In *Cross Creek Cookery* Mrs. Rawlings'
recipe suggests adding 2 tablespoons lemon juice or
vinegar for every pound of frog legs.) Simply dip
lightly in flour or cornmeal, fluffing with the fingers.
Shake off the excess flour.

For the frog legs, fluff first in flour, then dip in milk,
and again in flour. The catfish and cooter need to be
dipped only in flour or cornmeal. Mrs. Herman
recommends deep fat frying for catfish, preferably
dipped in cornmeal first; pan frying for cooter fluffed
in flour, and deep fat frying for frog legs. Fry to a
nice golden brown.

Serves: allow 6–8 oz. per serving
Preparation: 5–10 minutes plus 1 to 4 hours chilling
             for cooter or frog legs; 5 minutes for
             catfish (after cleaning)
Cooking: 5–6 minutes for catfish or frog legs;
             45 minutes for cooter

*"In Cross Creek Cookery, Mrs. Rawlings suggests
adding a whole beaten egg and fine bread crumbs to
the flour. And instead of oil for frying, she used
Dora's butter, a rich, flavorful butter from a favorite
Jersey cow."*

Lake City People, Lake City, Florida, in the middle 1880s (Florida State Archives)

Johnson's

Cedar Key

A century ago, with a population of 5,000, Cedar Key was Florida's second largest city. Before the Civil War there was a booming railroad connection—the first major one in the state—with Fernandina Beach, on the east coast. Eberhard Faber had begun to develop a sawmill for shipments to his New Jersey pencil factory.

But as with so many small towns of 19th-century Florida, boom days were followed by busts. Over the years the population dwindled to about 800. Cedar Key is now a town where people come to slow down, to unwind. Madge Johnson, a Cedar Key resident virtually all her life, will tell you there's not much to do except go fishing, clamming or crabbing, hunting, or operate a restaurant.

Indeed, operating her own restaurant is how she and her sister, Catheryn Gautreau, spend their time. They also have a fish market, downstairs from the restaurant. Other family members help out in both businesses.

"This little restaurant is like an American dream," Madge says. For many years she had helped her husband gather and produce seafood dishes. She even took their fishing boat out alone on occasion, something that many women didn't often do, she says.

There's an almost mystical sense about the Cedar Keys that makes one feel secure, even though the town is so remote from any other city. Some believe the atmosphere affects the flavor of the seafood. But Madge explains that the combination of fresh and salt water in three bodies of water causes the oysters, for example, to grow at tremendous speed. They already have a salty taste, so you don't need to add more. Typically, the soft-shelled crabs available here* are tender and sweet. Another local specialty is red fish chowder, but if red fish isn't available, grouper may be used as a substitute.

The atmosphere at Johnson's is casual, as is everything about Cedar Key. But there's nothing casual about the size of the servings. "No one goes away hungry," Madge says, "but I don't know how they eat it all!" Actually, the "half dinners" are plenty and are popular among those with less hearty appetites.

The house specialty is called the Molly Brown Special. It's in such great demand that as many as 75 private planes a day have been known to fly in to pick up these dinners. It's a four-course feast which includes a seafood cocktail, stone crabs, Cedar Key's famous hearts of palm salad (popularly known as swamp cabbage), and a heaping plate of assorted seafood. Small wonder!

Directions: From U.S. 19/98 North or South, take SR 24 West at Otter Creek. It's 23 miles to Cedar Key along an almost totally undeveloped straight stretch of road through clumps of sabal palm, cypress, and cedar. The road is unlit. Once you get to Cedar Key, follow signs to the pier. The whole island is only about a mile long and a half-mile wide, so you'll have a hard time getting lost.

While you're here: The Cedar Key State Museum is a little less than two miles north of SR 24 and contains exhibits of household artifacts from the town's past. If you're in town mid-April for the annual Cedar Key Art Festival or mid-October for the Seafood Festival, you'll see an otherwise sleepy village wake up and take on an animated character. The art festival is one of the best known in the state. The seafood festival includes an oyster-shucking contest and a parade.

*To order fresh, Cedar Key soft-shelled crabs, write to James Allen Seafood, General Delivery, Cedar Key, FL 32625. Tell him we sent ya!

CRABFINGERS

---

1   1-lb. package crabfingers, steamed
2   eggs
    water
    dry, light cornmeal

Beat eggs in a small bowl with a fork until smooth, adding about three parts water to eggs. Roll crabfingers lightly in cornmeal and dip a few at a time in eggs with one hand. Hold cornmeal in other hand and squeeze around dipped crabfingers. Fry until golden brown, and serve with tartar or cocktail sauce.

Serves: 3
Preparation: about 5 minutes
Cooking: about 5 minutes per batch

"Crabfingers are also known as cocktail claws. They're whole crab claws with the shells peeled off. Dipping in meal, then eggs, then meal again makes a nice, light breading."

HEARTS OF PALM SALAD

---

1   head lettuce
    sliced peaches, canned or fresh—3 slices per
    serving
2-3 cans hearts of palm*, sliced, or fresh if available
    sugared dates for garnish
1   large can pineapple chunks
    ice cream topping, below

Place lettuce in individual salad bowls and arrange
fruit around sides, with hearts of palm in center. Top
with:

ICE CREAM TOPPING (make ahead)

½   gal. plus 1 qt. vanilla ice cream
7   oz. pineapple juice
4   T. mayonnaise
1   T. crunchy peanut butter (a little goes a long
    way!)
⅓   t. green food coloring

Combine all ingredients and beat with mixer to a
working consistency, taking care not to let ice cream
get too soft or it will crystallize. Refreeze. Serve
when firm enough to scoop, about 3 hours.

Serves: 6-8 (makes ¾ gallon)
Preparation: 15 minutes plus freezing time

*"Nearly everyone has a favorite hearts of palm dish,
but the ice cream topping makes this one special!
Fresh hearts of palm are available within limitations
spelled out by state law (see Appendix)."*

*Available in most Gourmet Specialty Shops.

Miami River Picnic at Fergeson Place, Florida (Florida State Archives)

Masaryktown Hotel Restaurant, Masaryktown, Florida

Masaryktown Hotel Restaurant

Masaryktown

In contrast with the ethnic communities that have become assimilated into modern city life, Masaryktown is a good example of a small town that continues to focus on the Old Country's customs. Named for the first president of the Republic of Czechoslovakia, it was first settled in the 1920s. The original intent of the Czech immigrants who formed the Hernando Plantation Company was to raise citrus to sustain the community. But two killer freezes wiped out so much of the crop that many of the men returned to New York, their port of entry into this country, to raise capital instead.

Those who stayed, however, turned to chicken farming, an enterprise which became so successful that there were once as many as 50 farms in the area. Now there are only about 15 farms, and the owners are a large Tampa corporation instead of individual Czech and Slovak-Americans. Chicken dinners are still a traditional favorite, and the Masaryktown Hotel Restaurant is a friendly place for the family. Both Czech and American cooking are offered.

Established in 1925 as a hotel, the building is a simple white frame structure. Today it's no longer a hotel, but owner Harold Schaefer and his family live upstairs. Go past the entry foyer and gift shop to the dining rooms, where the sound of conversation creates a pleasant ambiance. The rustic wood paneling is a backdrop for some earthy Czech sayings in picture frames.

The menu features different specials every day. The *Halusky* that's served with the *Chicken Paprikash* is a noodle dish similar to the German *Spaetzl* and has a doughy texture that comes from keeping the lid on the pot while it's being cooked. Many typical Czech recipes call for extra sugar, like their carrots, which are also seasoned with chives. Harold says their popular strudel dessert is made by one of the older women in the town who won't reveal the recipe. But, he adds, there are other cooks to carry on the tradition when she's gone. Try the *Kolacky,* too, a pastry not quite so flaky as the strudel. Czech kitchens usually contain a *Pirka*, or goose-feather baster, to brush over the pastries.

Throughout the year festive dance celebrations are held at the new Masaryktown Community Hall, especially for Masaryk's birthday and Czech Independence Day (October). The Beseda Dancers wear traditional Czech folk costumes with bright colors, intricate designs, and rickrack. You can buy tickets at the Masaryktown Hotel Restaurant and see just how one of Florida's many ethnic groups has continued to keep its heritage alive.

Directions: *From Tampa, take U.S. 41 North, about 25 miles north of the Tampa city limits, just past the Hernando County Line (CR 578), to the blinking light at Wilson Boulevard. The restaurant is on the east side of the street. Or, coming from Brooksville, simply take 41 south about nine miles.*

While you're here: *This is a placid part of the state where back roads are dotted with flea markets and trading posts. It's a sort of year-round yard sale. Stop in and bargain—one person's junk is another's treasure! The* **Hernando County Courthouse** *in Brooksville is a distinctive red brick Victorian monument with a modern annex. In the early 1900s a fence was built around the building to protect the lawn from livestock.*

SAUERKRAUT

3½ C. sauerkraut (1 lb. 11 oz. can)
1   t. caraway seed
2   T. olive oil or cooking oil
¼   C. sugar
½   C. chopped onions
2   cups water (approx.)

Drain sauerkraut and place in pot or kettle. Add other ingredients and enough water to almost cover the mixture. Simmer until the onions are tender, about 20 minutes.

Serves: 4
Preparation: 5 minutes
Cooking: 20 minutes

"A quick and easy side dish for pork."

Masaryktown Hotel Restaurant
Masaryktown

CHICKEN PAPRIKASH

1   stewing hen or plump fryer
1   onion
    celery
1   clove garlic, chopped
    salt and pepper to taste
    paprika
½   C. salad oil or butter

Cook chicken in kettle, with or without the skin, in as little water as possible, with onions, celery, and salt and pepper to taste. (For bulk quantities the Masaryktown Hotel Restaurant bakes the chickens first, 20 at a time, then skins them and places in steam table trays.) After boiling, remove chicken and drain water after cooking. Bone when skin is cool. Coat bottom of deep frying pan with salad oil or butter and simmer remaining ingredients with chicken until chicken starts to brown. Watch oil carefully. Serve with:

SOUR CREAM SAUCE

2   C. sour cream
1   T. grated cheese (any kind—Colby or Cheddar or your choice)
1   small onion, chopped and sautéed
1   T. or more sugar to taste
1   t. to 1 T. chives
    salt and pepper to taste
    paprika

First warm the sour cream. Add cheese and blend in as it melts. Add onions, then seasonings. Sprinkle paprika on top. (If sour cream is too thick, thin the mixture by adding more milk.)

Serves: 4

Preparation: chicken—45 minutes; sauce—10
minutes

Cooking: depends on what kind of chicken is used.
Fryer takes about 45 minutes; stewing
hen takes about 2 hours.

**"A turnip or parsnip added to the chicken while
cooking adds a subtle sweet taste. Rather than
draining the water, reserve it to use as soup or
broth."**

—NOTES—

STUFFED CABBAGE

1   lb. ground beef
1   egg
1   small onion, chopped
1   small green pepper, chopped
¼   C. rice (raw)
    Lowry's seasoned salt
    salt and pepper to taste
    dash oregano
    dash sugar
1   large head of cabbage

ROLLS

Mix above ingredients (except cabbage) together with hands and set aside. Steam cabbage and pick 4 leaves off as they become pliable. Wrap ¼ lb. of meat mixture in each leaf. Then prepare the sauce.

SAUCE

1   6 oz. can tomato sauce
6   oz. water
    ham base or small piece blanched salt pork
⅛   C. chopped onions
2   T. sugar or to taste
    salt and pepper to taste

Mix all ingredients well. Pour over cabbage rolls. Bring sauce and cabbage rolls to boil, either on top of stove or in oven, until cabbage leaves are tender, about 45 minutes.

Serves: 4
Preparation: 30 minutes
Cooking: 45 minutes

"Ham base can be purchased at restaurant supply houses; however, you can replace it with salt pork with excellent results. Stuffed cabbage is a practical one-pot meal."

—NOTES—

SPICED APPLES

---

1   **1 lb. 4 oz. can sliced apples**
1   **t. cinnamon**
½   **C. sugar**
      pinch of salt to bring out flavor
1   **T. melted butter or margarine**
      water

Add enough water to mixture of above ingredients to barely cover them. Cook on medium heat until tender, about 10 to 20 minutes. Serve warm or cold, on the side with sauerkraut.

Serves: 4
Preparation: 5 minutes
Cooking: 20 minutes

"A delicious alternative to applesauce!"

Buddy Freddys

Plant City

Plant City's Johnson family has been in the food and restaurant business for more than 30 years. Brothers Buddy and Freddy Johnson are keeping alive this tradition in their own restaurant, a local landmark in its own right.

The fiddle mounted on the wall near the entrance belonged to their grandfather, "Pop" Johnson. Years ago, "Pop" used to entertain passersby on street corners in Montgomery, Alabama, and later performed with Hank Williams. The family moved to Florida in 1932 and has remained here ever since. Today one of the brothers' uncles performs at some of the family's anniversary celebrations.

The boys' father got started in the food business by hauling produce in east Florida. After he married and the boys were born, he ran a gas station that also served sandwiches on the south side of town. That small eatery eventually became a 250-seat restaurant located in downtown Plant City until just a few years ago. Mr. Johnson's sisters were the cooks.

Today, Buddy Freddys is a contemporary country restaurant just a block from Plant City's famous Strawberry Festival grounds. Surprisingly, the building used to be a drive-in, but it's now attractively decorated with rough-sawn cedar. Murals and small paintings by local artist John Briggs portray the rural and farm life of the area in bright colors. Briggs has been featured in *American Artist* magazine, has work in Washington's Hirshhorn Collection, and has received several grants and awards.

The menu at Buddy Freddys is an appealing mix of Southern and Florida recipes, many from within the family. Buddy is especially proud of their seasonal vegetable dishes. Breads and desserts are all homemade, and it's okay to place a take-out order.

Printed on the menu is a welcome to "our family of friends." This is a popular, in-town gathering spot where most of the locals know each other and don't hesitate to exchange news across tables. WIth that kind of friendly environment, even newcomers will feel at home at Buddy Freddys.

Directions: *Buddy Freddys is at 2104 West Reynolds Street (SR 574). From I-4 take Exit 11 (Plant City/Thonotosassa Road) south into town. The road bears slightly to the right just past SR 92 and becomes Lemon Street. Lemon Street intersects with Reynolds at the restaurant location. Buddy Freddys is on the northwest corner.*

While you're here: *The* **Strawberry Festival**, *combined with the* **Hillsborough County Fair**, *is a major popular event every February. Historically, Plant City was the site of a link in Henry Plant's railroad from Sanford to Tampa, completed in 1884.* **Florida Southern College** *is in Lakeland, about a 15- to 20-minute drive east. The attractive buildings were designed by Frank Lloyd Wright.*

COUNTRY FRIED STEAK

1   C. plain flour
1   t. salt
1   t. black pepper
6   5-oz. choice top round cube steaks
1   C. cooking oil

GRAVY

1   T. plain flour
½   t. Lawry Seasoned Salt
½   t. onion, granulated
½   t. granulated garlic
1   C. water

Combine flour, salt and pepper. Roll steaks in this mixture and fry in cooking oil until done. Set steaks aside. Save half of cooking oil. Combine dry gravy ingredients and add to pan. Stir over medium heat until brown. Add water and steaks. Simmer 15 minutes or until tender. Serve covered with gravy.

Serves: 6
Preparation: 5–10 minutes
Cooking: 15–20 minutes

"If you prefer, you can substitute 1 T. fresh chopped onion and 1 large chopped clove garlic for the granulated garlic. We also made this with some extra beef tenderloin tips we had on hand. Great!"

Buddy Freddys
Plant City

HOMEMADE CHICKEN AND DUMPLINGS

1   3-lb. chicken, fryer
2   qts. water
1   T. salt
1   t. black pepper
1   chicken bouillon cube
1   t. Lawry Seasoned Salt

DUMPLINGS

2   C. plain flour
3   large eggs
    water

Place chicken and all seasonings in a large pot and add water to cover. Bring to a boil. Skim residue from top. Lower heat and simmer until tender, about 45 minutes. Remove chicken. Cool, skin and bone. For dumplings, blend flour and eggs with enough water to form a stiff dough, like a pie crust. Pull off about a half cup of dough at a time and place on flour-dusted waxed paper. Dust top of dough with flour and roll thin, about ⅛ inch, with rolling pin. Cut into 1½-inch strips and pull off pieces about 1 inch long. Drop into boiling stock. Boil until dumplings are tender, about 10 minutes. Add chicken and simmer until heated through.

Serves: 6–8
Preparation: 20–30 minutes
Cooking: 50–60 minutes

"A classic Southern favorite."

FRESH ZUCCHINI AND TOMATOES

6   small fresh zucchini
1   clove garlic, smashed
1   8-oz. can of tomatoes, drained and diced (or 8 oz. fresh tomatoes, diced)
1   small onion, diced
1   T. Wesson oil
1   T. sugar
1   T. salt
½   t. black pepper
½   C. water

Cut zucchini into bite-size pieces. Combine with other ingredients. Simmer in a covered saucepan for 20 minutes or until zucchini is just tender.

Serves: 6–8
Preparation: 5–10 minutes
Cooking: 20 minutes

"Pass some grated Parmesan cheese for extra zip."

SCALLOPED EGGPLANT

---

2 large eggplants, peeled and cut into 1-inch x
    1-inch x 2-inch squares
1 C. grated sharp Cheddar cheese
1 8-oz. can tomatoes, diced
1 medium onion, diced
2 tubes Saltines, crushed
1 t. black pepper
1 t. salt
1 T. Wesson oil
1 t. oregano leaves
2 T. Parmesan cheese

Steam and drain eggplants. Combine all ingredients
except Parmesan cheese. Place in baking pan,
sprinkle Parmesan cheese on top, and bake 15
minutes at 400°F.

Serves: 8
Preparation: 10–15 minutes
Cooking: 15 minutes

"This is an easy way to prepare a hearty dish!"

STRAWBERRY SHORTCAKE

2   C. self-rising flour
1   t. baking powder
1   C. confectioners sugar
½   C. shortening such as Crisco
1   t. vanilla
1   C. milk
½   stick butter, melted
1   qt. fresh strawberries, sweetened to taste
     whipped cream

Combine and sift dry ingredients. Cut in shortening with pastry blender. Stir in vanilla and milk just until blended. It may be necessary to add a little more flour to achieve the right consistency. Form into a ball. Roll dough out about 1½ inches thick on floured wax paper or pastry cloth. Cut out biscuit-sized rounds with a lid from Pam or other spray can as a cookie cutter. Place biscuit rounds on a greased baking sheet. Bake at 350°F. for about 12 to 15 minutes or until golden brown. Brush tops with melted butter. Slice biscuits in half, add strawberries, and replace biscuit tops. Serve topped with whipped cream.

Serves: 6-8
Preparation: 15-20 minutes
Cooking: 15 minutes

"What better dish to come from Plant City, Florida's strawberry capital! This shortcake is sweeter than usual."

Florida Crackers cooking molasses, Dade City, Florida, 1912 (Tampa-Hillsborough County Public Library System)

P.Stockey

Allen's Historical Café

Auburndale

Veteran Florida songwriter and folksinger Frank Thomas penned a tune about Carl Allen, a native Floridian who was named by the statewide Sertoma Club as the state's Number One Cracker, "Polk County's favorite son."

Goes the song, "Carl Allen's my name and catfishin's my game / But that ain't all I've done. / I've been an old man and an old cow hand. / I'm a wise old son of a gun."

According to local folklore, that's what a Florida Cracker really used to be, a cow hunter, and Carl *was* one himself. During the 19th century the Cracker cowboys would crack their whips while they were out herding ridiculous-looking scrub cows. They were ridiculous-looking in those days, at least according to historical records, but by the 1920s, due to improvements in breeding technology, their appearance was much better. Cattle raising has been a Florida agricultural pursuit longer than in any other state in the country.

Now, Carl Allen, "Cracker," will let you in on many a piece of history, not only in the tales he can tell but also in the

99

café's decor. From the outside, Allen's Historical Café looks more like a pioneer outpost than a restaurant. Inside, every square inch of wall space is covered with memorabilia—fossils, plaques expressing folk wisdom, tools, antiques, and any other oddball treasure that seems to fit in. You can weigh yourself on an old-time scale and read your fortune. You can take pictures of someone hugging a big old stuffed bear that's often positioned outside the restaurant. (It's not the teddy bear kind either.) In the back room bluegrass bands hold weekly jam sessions, and you're welcome to join in with your own pickin' . . . or just grinnin', as the case may be.

The menu is pure "Cracker," too, with native specialties like cooter (soft-shelled turtle), armadillo, gator, and rattlesnake (that's right, rattlesnake!). Carl says his is the only restaurant in the state serving it. It's rather like fried chicken or frog legs but with less meat on the bone. Other regional trademarks aren't so exotic: dishes like the popular greens salad, made with avocado, pecans and purple grapes; and a yummy sweet potato pie for dessert. You can count on everything being freshly caught or grown and within the limits the law allows.

Allen's Historical Café is a crash course in regional food and state history that will keep you coming back for more!

Directions: Allen's Historical Café is at 1387 U.S. 92 West. From I-4 around Lakeland, take the U.S. 98 exit south. Turn east on U.S. 92 to the address, very near the Winter Haven Municipal Airport.

While you're here: All manner of bluegrass festivals take place in this area, including the state fiddling championship in March. The July 4 old-fashioned celebration includes, of all the unlikely phenomena, a Walking Catfish Race. You have to see it to believe it. Then skip on over to Winter Haven and see Florida Cypress Gardens for outstanding water-skiing shows, live animal exhibits, thousands of flowers, and hostesses dressed in Southern colonial-style gowns.

TURTLE SOUP

---

4   lbs. fresh turtle meat* or 1 lb. canned, if available
      enough water to cover
1   16-oz. can tomato juice
3-4   medium potatoes, peeled and cut into small
      chunks
½   lb. barley
1   large onion, cut into small slices
      salt, pepper and Accent to taste

Boil turtle until meat falls off bone, about 1½ hours.
Remove meat from broth. Remove all bones and cut
meat into bite-size pieces. Place meat back into
broth and add remaining ingredients. Simmer
2 to 4 hours.

Serves: 6-8
Preparation: 1½ hours
Cooking: 2-4 hours

*"If you use canned turtle meat, skip the 1½ hours of
pre-cooking and proceed with the rest of the recipe."*

*Some large supermarkets carry fresh-water turtle. It is the land turtle
that is illegal to catch in Florida during specified times of the year.
Check with the Game and Fresh Water Fish Commission (Appendix) for
which regulations pertain to which species.

CRACKLIN' CORN BREAD

1½ C. white or yellow self-rising corn meal
½   C. self-rising white flour
1   t. baking powder (level)
4   t. sugar
2   eggs
2   T. bacon grease
½   C. cracklings*
    about 1 C. buttermilk

Mix all ingredients except buttermilk. Add enough buttermilk to form a pouring consistency, like a cake batter. Pour into a hot, greased iron skillet or baking pan. Bake at 350°F. until done, about 20 minutes.

Serves: 4–6
Preparation: 10 minutes
Cooking: 20 minutes

"A standard Southern favorite. You don't need to add salt since the bacon grease and cracklings provide the flavor."

*Cracklings are made from the rind of ham or pork. You can buy them in the meat section of many supermarkets or make your own. Cut rind or fat into ½-inch squares. Place in a deep pan and bake at 300°F. until browned and all fat has been rendered. Drain and store in refrigerator for use as needed.

102

WATERMELON SOUP

2	qts. water
4-6	each, chicken breasts, necks, and backs for stock
	rind from 1 large watermelon (white portion only), cut into small cubes (about 4 C.)
1-2	medium carrots, cut into small cubes
1	C. onions, chopped fine
1-2	tomatoes, chopped fine
1	small can water chestnuts, drained and cut fine
	garlic powder, salt, black pepper, and Accent to taste

Make stock with chicken breasts, necks, and backs. When stock is done, remove breasts. Bone and remove all skin and fat. Cut breast meat into small cubes and set aside. Remove the rest of the chicken from the stock. You will be using only the breast meat in this recipe. Strain the stock. Add watermelon rind to stock and boil until rind is tender, about 30 minutes. Add carrots, onions, tomatoes, and water chestnuts, and boil until all ingredients are done. Add the cut-up chicken breasts and season to taste with garlic powder, salt, black pepper, and Accent. Serve with crackers.

Serves: 6-8
Preparation: 10 minutes
Cooking: about 40 minutes plus time to make
chicken stock

"This is a very light and delectable soup, perfect as an appetizer. If you are in a hurry, use canned chicken stock and poach the chicken breasts in it. Proceed as above. This recipe originated in the Philippines but works great with Florida watermelon!"

SWAMP CABBAGE

½   small head, heart of the cabbage palm*(cut out tender part inside the palm), or 2 cans hearts of palm*

6   slices smoked bacon, fried crisp ("sow's belly") salt and pepper to taste

1   C. water

Crumble the fried bacon and add to saucepan along with grease from bacon, water, and cabbage palm. Add salt and pepper to taste. Boil until tender. Simmer 3 to 4 hours.

Serves: 4–6
Preparation: 10 minutes
Cooking: 3–4 hours

"This is a delicious Florida dish with a taste all its own. Serve it as a vegetable. When the Spaniards came to Florida, they discovered that this native delicacy was a favorite with the Indians."

*Available at the Gourmet Section at your supermarket.

*See Appendix for information on legal use of this state-protected species.

FRIED CITRONS

2-3 unripe citrons (about the size of an orange)
salt, pepper and Accent to taste
flour for dipping
egg and milk beaten together, for dipping
cooking oil

Thinly slice citrons and soak in salt water about
2 to 3 hours, or longer if you prefer crisper citrons.
Season with salt, pepper and Accent. Dip in flour,
then in egg-milk mixture, then back in flour. Fry in
cooking oil as if you were frying tomatoes or
eggplant, until citrons are tender and brown.

Serves: 4-6
Preparation: 2 to 3 hours to soak
Cooking: 5-10 minutes

*"Carl Allen says this is a real treat, especially if you
like fried green tomatoes or eggplant. Citrons grow
wild in many regions of the state and can easily be
found in watermelon fields. This recipe actually is for
citron melons, which are green when they are young.
The larger white-and-green striped fruit is used to
make candied citron used in fruitcakes."*

SWEET POTATO PIE

1½   C. fresh or canned sweet potatoes, cooked
½   C. sugar
1   t. cinnamon
1   t. allspice
½   t. salt
2   eggs, beaten
1   C. evaporated milk
2   T. butter, very soft
1   9½-inch unbaked pie shell

If using canned sweet potatoes, drain. Mash potatoes
until free of lumps. Add sugar, cinnamon, allspice,
and salt. Mix well. Add beaten eggs and mix well.
Blend in milk and butter. Continue to mix until all
ingredients are well blended. Pour into unbaked pie
shell and bake for 45 minutes at 350°F. Serve hot.

Yields: 1   9½-inch pie
Preparation: 10–15 minutes
Cooking: 45 minutes

*"This is an old-fashioned recipe for an old-time
delicious pie. Add whipped cream or topping, if
you like."*

SWAMP CABBAGE AMBROSIA

½   head fresh swamp cabbage*, cut very fine, or
     1 can hearts of palm, drained and diced
1   large ripe papaya
8   oranges, peeled, seeded, and separated in
     sections
1   small package shredded coconut
1   small jar maraschino cherries
     sugar to taste (or sweetener of your choice)

Mix all ingredients and sweeten to taste. Chill
and serve.

Serves: 8–10
Preparation: 5–10 minutes plus 1–2 hours to chill

*"This is a very unusual way of preparing swamp
cabbage. Carl Allen suggests that you call several
days ahead if you wish to order a swamp cabbage
dish at the café to allow adequate preparation time
for the fresh plant."*

*See Appendix for information on legal use of this state-protected
species.

FLORIDA ORANGE PIE

1   C. sugar
5   T. cornstarch
2   T. orange rind, grated
1   C. fresh orange juice
1   C. orange sections, cut into pieces
3   egg yolks, beaten
1   T. lemon juice
1   T. butter
1   8-inch baked pie shell

Combine sugar, cornstarch, grated orange rind,
orange juice and orange sections. Cook on low heat,
stirring until clear. Add small amount of hot mixture
to beaten egg yolks, return to hot mixture, and cook
about 5 minutes longer. Remove from heat and blend
in lemon juice and butter. Pour into baked pie shell,
making sure both filling and shell are the same
temperature, either hot or cold. Top with:

MERINGUE

3   egg whites
6   T. sugar
¼   t. lemon extract

Beat egg whites until stiff. Beat in sugar and lemon
extract, beating slowly until smooth and glossy.
Spread on pie and bake at 400°F. until lightly
browned, about 8–10 minutes.

Yields: 1   8-inch pie (serves 6)
Preparation: about 15 minutes
Cooking: 8–10 minutes

"If you like a taste that is slightly more tart, reduce
the amount of sugar in the filling to ¾ of a cup. This
is an excellent way to get your 'taste of Florida
sunshine.'"

Acapulco Café, Zolfo Springs, Florida

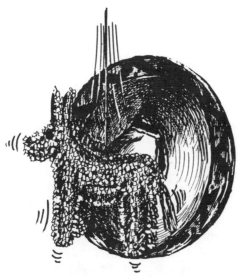

Acapulco Café

Zolfo Springs

"This is pretty much a second home to us," says Rose Zamora of her family's Acapulco Café. "We're here most of the time."

And the restaurant *does* look more like a large family room in someone's home than it does a restaurant. The TV set may be turned on, family pictures line the walls and knick-knack shelves, one dining area is paneled in knotty pine, and Mexican *piñatas* hang from the ceiling. There are only four tables in the main room, and even though this *is* a public place, it's cozy enough so that if you were seated on a couch instead of at a table, you could just slip your shoes off, lean back, and let Rose and her mother and sisters make you feel at home.

Rose was born in Brownville, Texas, and grew up in Helena, Arkansas, near the Mississippi River. Her mother had been a cook in several restaurants in Brownville. When they moved to Florida her father became a crew leader in the produce fields until his health no longer permitted him to work so hard outside. So, he opened the café in 1968. Since then, it's become known among locals as "the best place for

111

Mexican food outside Mexico," especially among those customers who themselves are produce workers from south of the border.

The chunks of fresh onions, tomatoes and lettuce in several of the dishes are far superior to the processed foods often used at many chain restaurants. Each of the flavors is distinctly fresh.

"We just serve what the people like," says Rose. "A paying customer needs to get their money's worth, so we don't take shortcuts."

What's essential to so many Mexican dishes, she says, are cumin seeds, Mexine chili powder, oregano, and garlic. Otherwise, it's "just ordinary food like you'd fix for yourself." And many of the recipes are good to prepare if you have to feed a large family or if you would rather fix one large batch and reheat part of it later.

Says Rose, "There's not much happening here (in Zolfo Springs), but you don't feel like the world's passing you by, either." Join Rose and her family for a meal, where the purple and white periwinkles create a colorful garden entrance for the Acapulco Café, year-round.

Directions: *The Acapulco Café is on U.S. 17 in Zolfo Springs, just south of the intersection with SR 64. The café is on the west side of the street. Zolfo Springs is about 50 miles east of Bradenton.*

While you're here: *Probably the most unusual "sight" in the whole state is Florida's "other magic kingdom," the home of sculptor* **Howard Solomon.** *Howard's home is literally his castle, sculpted out of sheet metal, complete with towers and turrets, art gallery, and "Medieval Campground." There are full outdoor recreational facilities. Though the castle is located in the "town" of Lily and the post office address is in Ona, you'll have to call directory assistance in Arcadia for the Solomon business phone to get directions to this* definitely *back-roads retreat. You can probably convince Howard to give you one of the "tours" he's famous for. About a half-hour's drive further east of Zolfo Springs is Sebring, home of the* **Coca-Cola Twelve Hours of Sebring** *auto racing classic held in the spring. And Arcadia, less than a half-hour's drive south, is the home of the oldest championship* **rodeo** *in the state and one of the best in the nation. You won't see any better Cracker cowboy "action" anywhere!*

GUACAMOLE SALAD

---

1 avocado, completely ripe
2 T. onions, finely chopped
½ medium tomato, finely chopped
  dash lemon juice (about ¼ lemon)
  pinch of salt
  lettuce cups or chopped lettuce
  tortilla chips (optional)
  Tabasco sauce (optional)

Peel avocado and mash until just lumpy. Do not blend smooth. Add onions, tomato, lemon juice, and salt. Serve on lettuce. Garnish with tortilla chips and pass the Tabasco or serve as a dip with tortilla chips.

Serves: 4
Preparation: 10 minutes

"If you are not going to use this salad right away, be sure to cover with plastic wrap and refrigerate. This makes an excellent dish with Mexican food or broiled steak."

Acapulco Café
Zolfo Springs

ENCHILADAS

SAUCE

1   cube butter or margarine
2   cloves garlic, minced
5   T. flour
2   t. chili powder
¾   C. cumin seeds, browned, or ground cumin
¼   t. oregano
    salt and black pepper to taste
2   C. water
½   C. tomato sauce

Melt butter in a large frying pan. Add garlic and
sauté. Stir in flour and cook, bringing mixture to a
gravy-like consistency. Blend in chili powder, cumin,
oregano, salt, and pepper. Add water and mix,
cooking over medium heat until mixture thickens and
comes to a boil. Taste and adjust seasonings if
necessary.

FILLING

1   lb. ground beef
1   medium tomato, finely chopped
1   medium bell pepper, finely chopped
1   medium onion, finely chopped
1-2 cloves garlic, minced
    black pepper
1½ t. chili powder

Sauté ground beef in frying pan until halfway done.
Pour off fat. Add tomato, bell pepper, garlic, and
onion. Cook until vegetables are soft and meat is
brown, about 5 to 8 minutes. Add pepper to taste and
chili powder. Mix, and continue to cook a minute or
two until all ingredients are blended.

TORTILLAS

12 corn tortillas
    vegetable shortening for frying
1   medium raw onion, chopped
    Cheddar cheese, grated, for topping

If tortillas are frozen, thaw them completely. Heat
shortening in pan and fry each tortilla quickly, about
5 seconds on each side. Drain. Place tortilla in
baking dish, place meat mixture in middle, and roll
up. Line up enchiladas in baking pan, seam side
down. Pour sauce over all. Sprinkle chopped onions
on top, then grated cheese. Place in oven about
thirty minutes at 350°F., just long enough to heat
through. With a spatula, serve onto plates. This dish
is good accompanied by salad, Spanish rice, or
refried beans.

Serves: 4–6
Preparation: 30 minutes
Cooking: 45–60 minutes

*"There's nothing like homemade enchiladas, and this
dish is well worth the time. It's perfect to make
ahead and freezes very well. You can cook it, cool it,
then freeze it. Or, put it all together, minus the raw
onion topping, and freeze it. Add the raw onions just
before baking."*

MOLE DE GALLINA O PUERCO (CHICKEN OR PORK IN MOLE SAUCE)

---

1   chicken cut into serving pieces or 2 lbs. pork
        roast or chops
     water
     flour
     all-vegetable shortening
     chili powder
3   garlic cloves, chopped
     cumin seeds, browned in oil
     oregano
     salt and pepper
1   T. creamy peanut butter (not crunchy)

Cover chicken or pork with water and boil gently until cooked. Save the broth. Brown enough flour in shortening to form a gravy-like consistency. Add chili powder for color and blend well. Add garlic, cumin seeds to taste, then oregano to taste. Add salt and pepper to taste. Stir in enough of the reserved broth to make a gravy. Stir in peanut butter and keep stirring until completely combined. Add the chicken or meat and heat only long enough to heat the meat and to let the flavor of the sauce seep in. Serve with Mexican side dishes such as beans and rice.

Serves: 4–6
Preparation: 5 minutes
Cooking: about 35–40 minutes

"When you add the chili powder start with just a pinch so that it doesn't overpower the taste of the sauce. This is a variation on the traditional Mole Sauce which generally uses chocolate."

116

REFRIED BEANS

1   package (1 lb. 8 oz.) dry pinto beans
    water to soak
    cumin seeds to taste
    salt to taste
    vegetable shortening

Follow instructions on package of dry pinto beans
for soaking and cooking. Drain. Heat shortening in
pan, then add beans. Cook briefly and mash fine
while cooking. Keep stirring over low heat until
beans are completely refried.

Serves: 8
Preparation: 10 minutes plus 3–3½ hours for
                soaking and cooking beans
Cooking: about 30 minutes

*"Cook up a batch and store in refrigerator or freezer,
re-heating as needed. You'll know when they're
done—they'll smell terrific!"*

Latam Restaurant

Tampa

How often do you find a *young* restaurant owner who's assured, outgoing, competent, and already has 15 years of experience under his belt? Not very, and that's why David Morejon is unusual.

David was 12 when his mother and father opened the Latam Restaurant in 1968, and he grew up in the business, doing everything—waiting on tables, cashiering, bartending, cooking, even scrubbing floors. He was all set to go to law school in Texas but instead took advantage of the opportunity to become a partner in the family business in 1978.

"I had a good teacher," David says, "my dad. He was the chef at the Spanish Park Restaurant for 18 years. And the bartender here was Dad's master chef. My uncle was a chef at the Columbia Restaurant. All the masters in Tampa were my teachers."

That training, combined with the low overhead of a long-term building lease and careful management, has enabled David to carry on the family traditions of outstanding Latin and American cooking at reasonable prices. The Latam doesn't charge much more than cost plus something to cover time and a modest profit, yet you'll find both common and unusual dishes, local and imported seafood, and fresh beef. The *Picadillo*, for example, is made with filet mignon instead of ordinary ground beef because the restaurant does its own butchering and grinding. The meat is purchased from Florida's own giant conglomerate, the Lykes Company.

David says the differences between Spanish and Cuban cuisine are as much in the menu items as in the preparation. A typical Cuban meal, for example, may include roast pork, *Moros* (black beans and rice), and *Yuca with Garlic Sauce*. One of the popular Cuban dishes he and one other cook prepare is *Pollo Real Campina*, named after an old town in Cuba. It's a savory baked chicken entree with garlic, olive oil, onions, thick potato slices, and paprika. Spanish dishes are more likely to be spicier and hotter.

Another famous and easy-to-make dish is *Steak Milanesa*. Pound a steak fillet thin, bread it, deep fry, and serve with a tomato sauce with peas, chopped egg, and pimiento or parsley for decoration. *Chicken Valenciano* is cooked with beer and *chorizo* (Spanish sausage).

Some of the traditional Spanish and Cuban dishes such as *Paella* and *Boliche* are served at the Latam, but David says some people feel they are either too time-consuming for average home preparation or require special techniques that are somewhat complicated.

But whatever your taste preference, Latin or American, you'll find plenty to please you at Latam.

Directions: The Latam Restaurant is at 2511 West Columbus Drive. From I-275 take the Howard Avenue exit and head north. Turn left (west) on Columbus Drive, one block to address at the intersection with Armenia Avenue. The Latam is on the northwest corner.

While you're here: Drive east on Columbus and south on Boulevard into the **Old Hyde Park** *area, a mostly residential neighborhood with attractive restored old homes. Where stately mansions line* **Bayshore Boulevard**, *overlooking Hillsborough Bay, you'll probably see many joggers along the road. Closer in to town is the* **University of Tampa**, *housed in what was formerly the* **Tampa Bay Hotel**, *built by developer Henry Plant a century ago. Its graceful mosques are the most distinguishable feature of Tampa's skyline. One wing of the main building is now a historical museum.*

GARBANZO BEAN SOUP

(Allow time to soak beans overnight)

1   16-oz. can garbanzo beans
2   cans water

SOFRITO (lightly fried ingredients):

oil
¼   lb. tocino (salt pork cut in pieces)
1   chorizo (Spanish sausage)
¼   lb. ham
1   potato, cut in small cubes
1   onion

pork bone (Boston butt)

Soak beans overnight. Add salt, but be careful with amount, using only enough to help soften the beans. Drain salt water. You may want to soak them again in plain water to reduce the salty taste. Boil several hours until soft. Then add sofrito and pork bone. Simmer and serve as needed.

Serves: 3–4
Preparation: 10 hours
Cooking: 3–4 hours

"This is the traditional way to prepare this popular soup."

TENDERLOIN TIPS SALTEADOS

cooking oil
1   lb. tenderloin beef tips, cut into ½-inch chunks
    salt and pepper, to taste
½   onion, chopped
½   green pepper, finely chopped
1   clove garlic, chopped
1   large potato, diced and sautéed until brown
¼   C. mushroom stems and pieces
⅛   C. sherry
½   C. brown gravy or beef stock

Coat bottom of frying pan with cooking oil. Heat oil, add meat, and sauté until brown. Add remaining ingredients and cook until onions, peppers and meat are cooked through, about 20 minutes.

Serves: 4
Preparation: 10 minutes
Cooking: 25-30 minutes, including time to sauté
              diced potatoes

"Serve with rice and a green vegetable. We added a handful of almonds to the leftovers after reheating."

Latam Restaurant
Tampa

STEAK À LA DAVID

SAUCE

(makes 1 pint—enough leftovers for
6-8 servings)
4 oz. dry red wine
¼ lb. butter, cut in small pieces
¼ C. beef bouillon
juice of 1 lemon
¼ C. water
⅓ C. Lea & Perrins Worcestershire sauce
(or your favorite brand)

STEAK

10 oz. fillet
bread crumbs
cooking oil
⅛ C. mushrooms, sliced (sautéed if desired)
1-2 slices Swiss cheese
¼ C. onions, chopped fine
2 sprigs parsley, chopped
2 T. peas, cooked
pimiento for garnish

For sauce, mix all ingredients together and bring to a
boil. Keep warm while steak is cooking. Pound steak
with mallet to flatten. It should still be somewhat
thick. Bread fillet and deep fry to desired level of
doneness (about 5 minutes for a 1-inch thick fillet,
rare). Set fillet in ovenproof dish or metal pan.
Sprinkle mushrooms over top and place slices of
Swiss cheese over mushrooms. Bake in oven
for 2 minutes at 350°F., just long enough for cheese
to melt. Sprinkle parsley and onions on top, then
peas and pimiento. Pour 1½ to 2 ounces of sauce
over each serving of steak.

Serves: 1 (Sauce 6-8 persons)
Preparation: 20 minutes
Cooking: 10-15 minutes

*"This recipe is David's own adaptation of what
S. Agliano of Agliano Seafood meant when he said,
'I want a big steak and I want it breaded and tender.'
Surprisingly, this dish is not at all greasy. The
breading and quick frying keep the juices in and the
fat out."*

—NOTES—

SEAFOOD À LA VASCA

½   lb. small shrimp (or larger shrimp cut up),
     cooked, peeled, and deveined
½   C. mushrooms, sliced and lightly sautéed
12 oz. fish fillet such as whiting, lightly sautéed
4   oz. crab meat, cooked and picked over for
     shells and cartilage
8   large scallops, cooked (can be cut in half)
     Bechamel Sauce

In an oven-proof dish, arrange shrimp for a bottom layer. Place mushrooms over the shrimp. Place fish fillets over mushrooms, then the crab meat. Arrange scallops on each side. Prepare the Bechamel Sauce.

BECHAMEL SAUCE

4   T. butter
¼   C. onions, finely chopped
½   t. salt
½   t. white pepper
2   C. milk
1½-2 T. flour
1   raw egg
      paprika
      melted butter to pour over fish
      parsley and pimiento for garnish

Melt 4 T. butter and sauté onions, being careful not to burn. Add salt and pepper. In another pot, heat milk and bring just to the boil. Stir in flour to butter-onion mixture to make a thick paste. You may have to add more butter. Cook, stirring until mixture is smooth. Add milk and mix until there are no lumps. Heat, continuing to stir until mixture is thickened. Add raw egg and mix well. Pour sauce over fish.

Sprinkle paprika on top; then pour over a little melted butter. Bake at 350°F. until sauce is browned, about 5 minutes. The fish is already cooked, and the baking is just for warming and to bring out all the flavors. Garnish with parsley and pimiento.

Serves: 4
Preparation: 20 minutes
Cooking: 20 minutes (includes time for cooking fish and Bechamel Sauce)

"This is a mouth-watering dish with a mild sauce. Try adding a little chopped fresh basil, oregano or other herb to the sauce for variety and color."

—NOTES—

YUCA CON MOJO DE AJO
(YUCA WITH GARLIC SAUCE)

1   package frozen yuca (available in Spanish
      groceries)
      water to cover
      salt to taste

Thaw frozen yuca. Place in pot and cover with water.
Add a little salt and boil until soft (similar to
preparing boiled carrots or potatoes), about
15 minutes.

GARLIC SAUCE: (makes 1 quart)

1   pt. pork lard (rendered after cooking pork)
½   pt. clove garlic, chopped fine (dehydrated garlic
      may also be used), or less, to taste
1   whole onion, chopped
      juice of 1 whole lemon
      salt and pepper to taste
1-2 oz. dry white wine or cooking wine
1   oz. vinegar (optional)

Mix pork lard and garlic. Add onion, lemon juice, salt
and pepper to taste, and wine. Add vinegar if desired.
Heat mixture until it boils. It will take several
minutes for the garlic and the onions to cook, but be
careful not to let them burn. Serve over yuca, roast
pork, or other dishes for which you would like a
sauce with a very strong garlic flavor. Leftover sauce
can be refrigerated and re-heated.

Serves: 4–6
Preparation: yuca—10 minutes; sauce—5 minutes
Cooking: yuca—15 minutes; sauce—5-10 minutes

"Garlic lovers, this is for you!"

La Teresita

Tampa

When Latin families enter the restaurant business, they do so *con gusto*—all the way. For Max Capdevila, his four sons, and several others in the family, La Teresita is indeed their life. What started out as a small grocery store expanded by adding a fish market. Next came a sandwich shop and later a full café that's packed morning to night. They're all part of La Teresita's operation. The grocery store, which is less than half the size of a typical chain supermarket, offers just as much of what the local Hispanic community wants, often at better prices.

The café is simply designed, with counter space only. But just wait until they start piling the food high on your plate. An order for one can often satisfy two, for less than what you'd pay at a fast food restaurant. And the food here offers a taste of genuine ethnic flavors along Tampa's "Boliche Boulevard." That's Columbus Drive's nickname because of the large number of Cuban and Spanish eateries and stores that line the street for several blocks.

Says George, the oldest son, "There's nothing better than competition. All the restaurants on Boliche are always packed."

You can easily observe what this part of the community is like at La Teresita. Not quite half of the customers are Anglos, says George. The mayor stops in frequently for *Café con Leche*. There's a reason to drink it sweetened. It's extremely strong-flavored Cuban coffee mixed with milk that has been steamed in a separate container.

"There's nothing quiet about Latins," George observes as he surveys the animated conversations across the counter. "And Latins *eat*."

La Teresita serves both Cuban and Spanish dishes, but George says the differences are mainly in the seasonings. In Cuba, he explains, black beans go with white rice, not yellow; and here, white rice on the table is a must for his Cuban customers. Many recipes call for juice from sour oranges, a variety that some of his customers bring in from their own backyards. It doesn't have as strong an acid taste as lemon juice, which is sometimes used as a substitute. The *Bistec Palomilla* is a popular meat dish. It's one that in typical Cuban fashion calls for thinly sliced sirloin that is pounded even thinner, seasoned, pan fried, and served with a heaping portion of yellow rice. Generally, says George, the Latin diet doesn't have so many green vegetables as does an Anglo diet but focuses more on potato-like roots such as yuca and malanga.

One thing's for certain—no one ever leaves La Teresita hungry!

Directions: La Teresita is at 3202 West Columbus Drive. From I-275 take the Howard Avenue exit and head north. Turn left (west) on Columbus Drive, seven blocks to address. La Teresita is on the south side of the street.

While you're here: Tampa is a very sports-minded city, and you're only a few minutes away from **Tampa Stadium**. Catch a pro NFL, USFL, or NASL game with the Tampa Bay Buccaneers, Bandits, or Rowdies, respectively. Then drive out to the **Tampa International Airport**, so well-designed that it has become the model for airports in many other cities. For another view of the urban landscape go up to the observation deck.

QUICK GARBANZO BEAN SOUP

---

1   onion
2   small or 1 large green pepper
1   clove garlic
1   chorizo (Spanish sausage)
½   C. Vigo olive oil (or your favorite brand)
1   16-oz. can of garbanzo beans (chick peas),
      drained
2   cans water
½   lb. cooking ham (smoked ham or ham hock) cut
      into small cubes
½   t. salt

Cut onion, peppers, garlic, and chorizo into small pieces. Sauté in olive oil until vegetables are limp. While vegetables are sautéing, mix garbanzo beans and water in a saucepan and heat. Add sautéed vegetable mixture, smoked ham or ham hock, and salt and mix. Bring to a boil. Reduce heat and simmer for 15 minutes.

Serves: 3–4
Preparation: 15–20 minutes
Cooking: 20–25 minutes

"This is a delicious soup that the whole family should enjoy. The chorizo gives the soup a special flavor that complements the garbanzo beans. Serve with a tossed green salad and hot crusty Cuban or French bread."

PALOMILLA STEAK

top butt steak, thinly cut
Adobo Criollo seasoning* (all-purpose seasoning
    with salt, pepper, garlic, and onion powder)
pork lard or oil
chopped onions
lemon juice or sour orange juice (optional)

Pound steaks to tenderize. Sprinkle lightly or to taste
with Adobo seasoning. If desired, sprinkle with
lemon or sour orange juice. Fry in pork lard or oil on
both sides until done, about 5 minutes. Onions can
be fried with steak or served raw and sprinkled over
top. This is best prepared well-done.

Serves: allow 6–8 oz. per serving
Preparation: 10 minutes
Cooking: 5–10 minutes

*"We suggest that you use oil rather than pork lard if
you are unfamiliar with the taste."*

*Available in most supermarkets

BISTEC EMPANIZADO MILANESA

1   C. spaghetti sauce (your favorite recipe or a
     prepared sauce such as Ragu)
     Parmesan cheese to taste
2   eggs, raw
     about ¼ C. milk
1   pkg. Vigo flavoring/coloring (or your favorite
     brand)
4   thinly cut top butt steaks (same as for
     palomilla)
     bread crumbs
     oil for frying
2   eggs, hard boiled
     parsley, chopped
     red pimiento, chopped
1   C. peas, cooked

Heat spaghetti sauce with Parmesan cheese in a
saucepan. Keep warm while you prepare the steaks.
With a fork, beat raw eggs, milk, and Vigo flavoring/
coloring in a bowl. Dip steaks in bread crumbs, then
in egg and milk mixture, and again in bread crumbs.
Pound steaks lightly so that bread crumbs will
adhere. Fry breaded steaks quickly, just a minute or
so on each side. Remove steaks to platter. Spread
heated spaghetti sauce over the top. Garnish with
crumbled hard-boiled eggs, parsley, pimiento, and
cooked peas.

Serves: 4
Preparation: 10 minutes
Cooking: 8 minutes

*"This flavor combination is unique. Serve with a
tossed salad and spicy dressing and some crusty
Cuban bread."*

Mel's Hot Dogs

Tampa

Anyone who's ever eaten a kosher Vienna hot dog in Chicago knows what the real thing is. And you'll recognize it in no time flat at Mel's Hot Dogs in Tampa, because that's what is served—kosher Vienna hot dogs from Chicago. That's where owner Mel Lohn comes from himself.

How he came to Tampa and landed in the restaurant business is a story in itself. In the early 1970s Mel was a saxophone player with a rock band that was touring in the Tampa Bay area. When their gig was over, everyone returned to the Midwest except Mel, who stayed because he loved the sunshine. (Where have you heard *that* before . . .?) But because no other restaurant served "red hots" (kosher Vienna hot dogs) in Tampa, he did the only thing he *could* do and went into the business as Mel's Red Hot Ranch.

When all his customers—whom he calls on a first-name basis—called the place, simply, Mel's Hot Dogs, he too adopted the name. Mounted and framed on the walls of the restaurant are praises of the hot dog (which he claims is superior to the hamburger) and recognition for his own efforts on behalf of the wiener. Browse around and chuckle at

132

the cartoons and caricatures and pithy sayings about "dogs." ("Have a wienerful day" is typical.) It's great entertainment.

What makes Mel's hot dogs so succulent is their natural casing. Whole beef cuts are stuffed inside by hand and then slowly smoked. When you bite down, your teeth pierce this casing and it "pops." You get a mouthful of well-seasoned meat. This is considerably different from the ordinary kind of skinless hot dog made with meat (not necessarily beef) and fillers or extenders. If you've never eaten a kosher-style frank before, you're in for a treat. Be sure to insist on the bright green relish for a garnish—it's the best we've tasted.

Actually, even if you *have* savored this kind before, you're still in for a treat because Mel's version has been declared *top* dog in the world by no less a connoisseur than an ABC news rep who praised Mel's while touring in Europe.

Dig it, (hot) dog lovers!

Directions: Mel's Hot Dogs is at 4136 East Busch Boulevard. Take the Busch Boulevard exit east from I-75 north or south. Mel's is on the north side of the street. Busch Gardens is about one mile west.

While you're here: The state's second most popular tourist attraction next to Walt Disney World is **The Dark Continent, Busch Gardens**. Besides the re-creation of yesterday's Africa, don't miss the original tropical garden area, cultivated on land that once was arid and barren. Nearby is the park's **Adventure Island** for waterslide fun and other water amusements for the whole family. Just another mile to the north is the **University of South Florida** campus, which celebrated its 25th anniversary in 1982. Major athletic events and popular entertainment are offered at the University **Sun Dome**. Just down the street from the main campus entrance is the **Museum of Science and Industry**, with "hands-on" exhibits for all ages.

REAL CHICAGO-STYLE HOT DOG

---

1   pure beef natural casing hot dog (preferably
      made by Vienna Sausage Manufacturing
      Company, Chicago)
1   oversize rectangular-shaped poppy seed bun
      yellow mustard
      sweet Spanish onions, diced
      bright green hot dog relish (called "piccalilly" in
      the Midwest)
1   medium cured kosher dill pickle, thinly sliced
      celery salt
      sweet, ripe tomato, thinly sliced
      water

Heat water in saucepan to 190°F. Place hot dog in
heated water and cook until it rises to the top, about
two and a half to three minutes depending on
whether it's frozen or already thawed. Then cook an
additional 30 seconds after it has risen and remove
promptly. Place in freshly steamed* hot dog bun.
Spread with mustard and onions to taste, a light
topping of relish, tomato slices, and a light sprinkling
of celery salt. Top off with dill slices. Serve with
french fries and barrel-cured (not canned) sauerkraut,
heated if you like.

Serves: 1
Cooking: 5 minutes

*"Mel adds, tongue in cheek, 'Wrap in a dirty brown
bag . . . and enjoy!' Also, a Chicago-style hot dog is
never served with catsup."*

---

*Steamed buns are popular in Florida; try them toasted as an alternative.

134

MEL'S FRENCH FRIES

**Grade A extra fancy Idaho potatoes, sliced and
cut in strips.**
Pure Grade A vegetable shortening or oil

Heat oil in skillet to 375°F. Immerse small amounts of
potatoes at a time for two and a half to three minutes
until golden brown. Remove and drain. Salt to taste.

Yields: 1 potato per serving
Cooking: 5-10 minutes depending on number of
servings

*"Mel adds, also tongue in cheek, 'No hot dog worth
its buns is ever served without French fries.' "*

Silver Ring Café

Ybor City (Tampa)

Mention Tampa to your friends and chances are the symbols they'll think of first will be cigars and Cuban sandwiches.

The two go hand in hand, especially in Ybor City, called the "cradle of Cuban liberty" by historians because of the role José Martí played during Cuba's struggle for independence from Spain. In 1886, following a recommendation from a colleague from Key West, Vicente Martínez Ybor established a cigar factory in Tampa when labor problems with his Key West plant became troublesome. During the 1890s, Martí was an outspoken and eloquent patriot for the cause of Cuban freedom. He was killed in a skirmish in Dos Ríos. The historic events of the turn of the century—the Spanish-American War, the culmination of Cuba's fight for freedom, Ybor City's boom-town days and, later, strikes in the cigar industry—contribute much to Tampa's rich and colorful heritage.

As late as the middle 1900s, the streets of Ybor City were filled with stores that stayed open until midnight, dozens of active restaurants, and girls hawking deviled crabs and hot chestnuts.

So recalls Angelo Cacciatore, owner of the Silver Ring Café since 1936. "There was a lot of action . . . it was real Latin-y," he reminisces, something like Little Italy in New York.

Even though the community has lost many of its former residents due to urban pressures, the district is undergoing a period of urban renewal that should fully restore its vitality in a few years.

Since 1936, Angelo and his staff have had the same menu, simple but consistent. Staples are Cuban sandwiches, *Pan con Mantequilla* (Cuban bread and butter), and Cuban coffee. The sandwiches are made fresh every day and are loaded with deli meats, cheese and pickles. You can watch the meat being sliced and the sandwiches being prepared through display windows streetside. Several thousand are made every week. The only time business ever slows down is at closing.

It's no surprise that the Silver Ring Café was a winner in the *Tampa Tribune's* Best Cuban Sandwich Contest and has been a finalist every year the competition has been held. Angelo insists that he gets the best bread and meat in town from the Casino Bakery and Four Star Meat Products, respectively. They've been supplying him for years.

By the way, if you're a baseball or a boxing fan, Angelo will have plenty of memories to share. He's personally been to 25 World Series games.

The Silver Ring Café would certainly be a major league contender in a World Series contest for Cuban sandwiches!

Directions: *The Silver Ring Café is at 1831 East 7th Avenue. From I-4 take the 22nd Street exit south. Turn right (west) on 7th Avenue to address. The café is on the south side of the street.*

While you're here: *Historic Ybor City is full of markers commemorating its exciting past. V.M. Ybor's original cigar factory is now* **Ybor Square***, a shopping and dining complex which includes fine antique and gift boutiques. With wrought iron grill work an integral part of their architectural design, social clubs for several different ethnic groups dot the streets. The Ferlita Bakery now houses the* **Ybor City State Museum***, containing the original 1896 ovens for baking Cuban bread and displays tracing the history of the town's cigar industry.*

CUBAN SANDWICH

---

1   loaf Cuban bread
1   lb. smoked ham, sliced thin
1   lb. roast pork, sliced thin
½   lb. salami, sliced thin
½   lb. Swiss cheese, sliced thin and cut into
    1½-inch strips
    pickle slices
    lettuce and tomatoes (sliced), optional
    mustard and mayonnaise to taste

Cut bread into quarters, about a foot long each. Slice open and place descending amounts of ham, pork and salami in layers along one half of bread. Spread two strips of Swiss cheese along length of sandwich and add pickle slices. Add lettuce and tomato if desired. Spread both sides of bread with mustard and mayonnaise to taste, and close sandwich. Warm for a minute to a minute and a half to get the outside of the bread nice and toasty, if you want.

Serves: 4
Preparation: 5–10 minutes

"Angelo makes two kinds of Cuban sandwiches: a regular one, which he serves with lettuce and tomato, and a special one, which he makes without lettuce and tomato but loaded up with three-quarters of a pound of meat. The loaves of bread are light as a result of more shortening being used during the baking process."

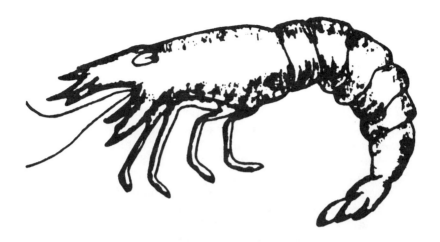

Paul's Shrimp

Tarpon Springs

What the conch is to Key West, the sponge is to Tarpon Springs. At least, that's true in terms of a local symbol. But sponging is more a matter of history now in this small, mostly Greek community in northern Pinellas County.

Some of that history is preserved in the decor of Paul's, famous locally for boiled shrimp since 1966. The original restaurant, a couple of doors down from the present enlarged location, featured almost life-sized murals of some of the folks in town engaged in traditional Greek customs. Painted with compassionate expressions, they're dancing at a *glendi* (festival) and stirring a pot of *Kavrouma* (a sort of meat stew) for the sponge divers to take on the boat. A map of "The Land of the Incredible Greeks" pinpoints which island each of the owners and his compatriots hailed from.

New murals liven the warm wood walls of the new Paul's, which Steve Tsalickis and his family have owned since 1979. Some of their family were in the original paintings, which you can still see if you ask them to point them out to you. Daughter Tula culled through magazines and private collections to find photos of Tarpon Springs community events from the 1920s through 1940s to become part of the counter decor at the bar.

But it's the boiled shrimp that Paul's is best known for. Order by the pound (about 25 to 30 shrimp per pound), and your plate will be served in the middle of the table, Greek-style. With everyone at the table sharing, there won't be anything wasted. With the succulent flavor of the shrimp enhanced by lemon juice and a touch of oregano, it's hard to imagine that there would be any waste anyway. Lightly fried smelts are also popular, and it's not uncommon for total strangers to become friends easily by passing their plates to nearby tables for samples.

The menu isn't extensive at this restaurant. It's not Greek in that you won't find *Pastitsio* or *Moussaka*, for example, both typical favorites. But it is Greek in the use of lemon juice, olive oil, and oregano for delicacies such as octopus. The same combination is likewise a delight with a conch salad that measures up to its Key West originator.

It should be no surprise that Paul's is popular not only among townsfolk but also with Italian customers, who identify with the country's Mediterranean location, and with regulars from around the Tampa Bay area, who became familiar with the restaurant after several newspaper reviews. The expanded building has helped take care of some of the lines, but you should know that even when the eatery first opened with only 10 tables and served only shrimp, people would wait two to three hours just for a pound of shrimp. They would write out their own checks at the bar.

You just can't keep a good thing down.

Directions: *Paul's Shrimp is at 514 Athens Street. From U.S. 19, turn west on SR 582 (Tarpon Avenue) and north to where it intersects with Alternate 19 (Pinellas Avenue). Turn left (west) about three-quarters of a mile further at Dodecanese Boulevard, as if you were going to the Sponge Docks, then left again in three blocks on Athens Street. Paul's is on the east side of the road.*

While you're here: The **Tarpon Springs Sponge Exchange and Docks** *are within walking distance. They're a colorful way to relive the excitement of what used to be a major industry until a blight during the 1940s reduced the growth of sponges. The* **Universalist Church** *features paintings by George Inness, Jr., son of the famous 19th-century artist. If you're in town on January 6, watch the* **Epiphany Celebration.** *Young men dive into the water, whatever its temperature, vying to retrieve a golden cross for good luck the rest of the year.*

—NOTES—

Paul's
Tarpon Springs

HORATIKI SALATA (Greek Peasant Salad)

16   slices feta cheese, 2 inches long
8-16   anchovies, whole or cut up
2-3   tomatoes, cut in chunks
1   large onion, sliced
1   large cucumber peeled, cut lengthwise, and
          halved
2   handfuls black olives
1   green pepper, sliced in rings
2   handfuls hot Greek peppers
        olive oil
        vinegar
        oregano

Arrange all ingredients in alternating order on plates, starting with the feta. Beat together 3 parts oil to 1 part vinegar and pour over salad. Sprinkle with oregano.

Serves: 4
Preparation: 10 minutes

"This is the true Greek salad without the lettuce that is called for in the Americanized version."

PICKLED OCTOPUS

(Allow time to marinate overnight)

5 lbs. octopus
   salt and pepper to taste
   vinegar
   water
1 C. cooking oil
½ C. lemon juice
1½ C. vinegar
   oregano
   fresh garlic, minced

Tenderize octopus by boiling in water with a little
salt and vinegar. When skin is soft (about 30 to
45 minutes) remove from water and cool. Clean skin
and remove slime. Cut octopus in small pieces. Place
in a bowl with oil, lemon juice, and vinegar making
sure that there are enough juices to cover meat. Add
a *little* oregano and garlic. Cover and marinate at
least 2 hours or overnight. Best when served the next
day.

Serves: 10
Preparation: about 1 hour (plus time to marinate)
Cooking: 30-45 minutes

*"Serve as an appetizer or buffet dish for a crowd.
You'll be a hit!"*

BROILED OCTOPUS

---

5   lbs. octopus (allow 6-8 oz. per serving)
    salt
    water
    vinegar
    cooking oil
    lemon juice
    lettuce, tomato slice, green pepper ring, olives,
       lemon wedge to garnish each serving

Boil octopus, as for pickled octopus (page 143). After cleaning, refrigerate and use as needed. Cut octopus into large chunks. Cover bottom of broiler pan with a thin film of cooking oil. Sprinkle octopus with lemon juice and place in pan with a little water. Broil until brown on each side, about 3-5 minutes. Add a little more lemon juice to the pan juices and serve over the octopus. Garnish each serving with lettuce, tomato slices, green pepper rings, olives, and lemon wedges.

Serves: 10-12
Preparation: about 1 hour
Cooking: 3-5 minutes

"This may be different, but be sure to try it. You're in for a nice surprise!"

CONCH SALAD

(Allow time to marinate overnight)

1	lb. raw conch meat, fresh or frozen
½	bunch scallions (both green and white parts), chopped
½	medium onion, chopped
1	medium tomato, chopped
½	bell pepper, chopped
¼	stalk celery, chopped
5	oz. oil
4	oz. vinegar
5	oz. lemon juice (about 3 lemons)
	dash black pepper
	oregano for garnish

Pound conch meat for 10–15 minutes to tenderize it. Cut into ½-inch pieces. Place in glass or pottery bowl. Add chopped vegetables, oil, vinegar, lemon juice, and black pepper. Mix well. Taste for seasoning. Marinate overnight or for at least 8 hours. Serve on a colorful plate. Sprinkle oregano to taste on top.

Serves: 4–6
Preparation: 20 minutes (plus marinating overnight)

*"This make-ahead dish is an elegant first course.
Serve it on a bed of lettuce with a parsley garnish. It
will make a conch-lover out of you!"*

The Chattaway

St. Petersburg

Years before the Sunshine Skyway Bridge linked St. Petersburg with Manatee County, there was the Chattaway Drive-In, a genuine drive-in that served only beer and wine. The little yellow wooden building housed a grocery store, a gas station, and a trolley stop. When Helen Lund bought it in 1950, she expanded it into a full-fledged restaurant without changing the exterior. Since then it's become a local historical landmark in a most picturesque setting.

The Coast Guard Station and the Army Reserve were much more active in St. Petersburg in the 1950s, and their personnel kept The Chattaway busy. Along came the passengers taking the ferry to Palmetto and the workmen who built the Skyway. That's when Helen began to prepare meals in earnest, to meet the construction workers' demands for "take-away" food.

Helen had no previous restaurant experience. "I used to work for Western Union pounding a typewriter," she reminisces. But she *did* entertain a lot at home, and every night she would think of something unique to prepare.

Although it began with just a fried chicken and hamburger menu (The Chattaway is still famous for its "Chattaburger"), the restaurant now features different daily specials as well.

The restaurant's ambiance perfectly fits the image of an earlier St. Petersburg. Bite into your burger under a graceful jacaranda tree shading your *al fresco* picnic table. You'll feel beachy at the shaded counter and bar. You'll feel Southern country nostalgic on the enclosed verandah or in the rustic old-time indoor dining room that has one of only two table-top shuffleboard games left in the city. Walls are decorated with English-born daughter-in-law Jill's collections from British travels—illustrations of famous buildings, souvenirs of the Royal Wedding, and plates from wherever.

You'll discover the "Other Florida" at The Chattaway in its very casual charm.

Directions: The Chattaway is at 358 22nd Avenue South. From I-275 head east at the 22nd Avenue South exit. The Chattaway is at the intersection of 22nd Avenue and 4th Street South, on the southeast corner. It's just across from the St. Petersburg Tennis Club, where Chris Evert-Lloyd and other famous tennis stars have trained.

While you're here: The restaurant is across the street from **Lake Maggiore**, *a popular site for relaxing and boat racing. The* **Boyd Hill Nature Trail** *is adjacent. Within minutes is the* **Salvador Dali Museum**, *adjacent to the St. Petersburg campus of the* **University of South Florida**. *The Dali Museum periodically rotates paintings and* objets d'art *from its collection. It's a major addition to the roster of fine arts resources in the Tampa Bay area.* **Bartlett Park**, *just across the street from The Chattaway, has an excellent tennis club, open to the public for a small fee.*

QUICK BARBECUE SAUCE

½   medium onion, chopped
¼   green pepper, chopped
½   clove garlic, minced
2   T. margarine
1   qt. catsup
1   T. chili powder
½   t. Tabasco sauce
⅛   C. vinegar
¼   C. sugar
⅛   C. Worcestershire sauce
    dash fresh pepper (or to taste)

Sauté onion, green pepper, and garlic in margarine. Add catsup and other ingredients. Mix well and simmer 15 minutes. Keep refrigerated in a tightly covered container—flavor gets better as you store.

Yields: a little more than a quart
Preparation: 15 minutes
Cooking: 15 minutes

"Helen Lund, The Chattaway's well-known owner, says that her customers adore this sauce. We strongly agree with her guests. Use for beef, pork, or chicken, or use your imagination."

AMERICAN SAUERBRATEN

5   lbs. boneless chuck
cooking oil for browning
salt
1   large onion, cut in chunks
2   C. vinegar
1   C. water
20 gingersnaps (more, if desired)

Brown meat on all sides. Add salt to taste and onions. After browning, add vinegar and water. Continue to add water until meat is done. Remove meat from sauce. Take 20 or more gingersnaps, soften with water, and add to gravy to thicken. Simmer 3 to 4 hours.

Serves: 10–12
Preparation: 5 minutes
Cooking: 4 hours

"Try to make this in advance so that you can skim off the fat and then re-heat the meat in the gravy. You'll enjoy this easy recipe with its continental taste."

Jack's Skyway Restaurant, St. Petersburg, Florida

Jack's Skyway Restaurant

St. Petersburg

The Navy didn't realize the specialized knowledge it was placing in the hands of Jack Thomas when he was a mess cook years back. Since that time, although he graduated from the University of Florida and pursued a successful career as an engineer with the Tampa Electric Company, Jack has never forgotten the standard Navy recipes and menus... with, of course, his own culinary improvements.

Jack's Skyway opened after a relative turned Jack on to O'Neill's Skyway Boat Basin. Jack purchased O'Neill's in 1976 and renamed it Jack's Skyway Restaurant. Since then he's captured distinguished fishermen, Canadians and even the London press, and just about everyone who's stopped in ever since.

Jack and his wife, Carol, continue to create exciting recipes. Their classics are based on what Jack learned about cooking eggs in the service and feature an assortment of omelets, breakfast delights, and the best chili. What he labels "Jack's S.O.S." is a tantalizing creamed sausage (use the extra hot) on a biscuit, not like what you might remember if you were in the service. This culinary entrepreneur is famous, too, for his pecan waffles, banana pancakes, home-made biscuits, and home-fried potatoes (great!).

It's easy to see why Jack's Skyway has become a Florida tradition. Though the restaurant seats only about 50 people, Jack is likely to serve about 1,000 biscuits a week, 2,500 eggs, 4,000 cups of coffee, 45 pounds of bacon, 100 pounds of sausage, and 400 pounds of potatoes. Hey, that ain't *small* potatoes!

Part of the experience of dining at Jack's is the nautical decor re-creating a ship's portholes and life preservers.

Jack welcomes you with a big grin. He'll chat a while and enjoy your company!

Directions: *Jack's Skyway Restaurant is at 6701 34th Street South. Take I-275 south as far as you can and follow signs to U.S. 19 to Bradenton when you exit. U.S. 19 is 34th Street; just follow it to the north end of the Sunshine Skyway. Jack's is just north of the toll plaza, on the west side of the street. Or, coming from Bradenton, follow U.S. 19 north, past the Skyway to the restaurant.*

While you're here: *The* **St. Petersburg Historical Museum** *(Haas Museum) re-creates the city's past and displays furnishings and items from old pioneer families. Also nearby is one of Pinellas County's most popular outdoor recreation areas,* **Fort DeSoto Park**. *The beach, picnic areas, and fishing are among the most pleasant in the area.*

BAKED BEANS "OLD NAVY BREAKFAST"

---

1   **46-oz. can of pork and beans, your favorite brand**
¾   **C. catsup**
½   **C. water**
⅔   **C. brown sugar**
2   **t. Worcestershire sauce**
4   **t. prepared mustard (Gulden's is good)**
⅓   **C. minced onion, fresh**
3   **strips smoked bacon or blanched salt pork, uncooked, cut into bite-size pieces**

Mix all ingredients well and place in a shallow dish or pan. Bake uncovered for 45 minutes at 325°F. Serve with corn muffins and pre-cooked smoked sausage, about 1-1½ inches in diameter (fried for best results).

Serves: 6–8
Preparation: 5–8 minutes
Cooking: 45 minutes

"These beans are good day and night."

FISHERMAN'S CHOWDER

1   46-oz. can of clam chowder
2   cans whole milk (use 46-oz. chowder can to
      measure)
1   qt. chowder mix* (see below), thawed
¾   cup cornstarch, dissolved in some of the above
      milk
1   t. white pepper
1   T. salt
1   T. MSG (monosodium glutamate)
      butter

Gently and thoroughly combine all ingredients. Cook
in a double-boiler or in a large pot over low heat for
about 1 hour. Stir frequently. Serve with a dollop of
butter on top of each serving.

Yields: 12–14 bowls
Preparation: 10 minutes
Cooking: 1 hour

*CHOWDER MIX

1   C. water chestnuts, sliced in ½-inch pieces
      (reserve liquid)
¾   C. clams, chopped in ½-inch pieces
1   C. raw boneless fish, cut in ½-inch pieces
1¼   C. canned yellow corn, undrained

*Jack's Skyway Restaurant
St. Petersburg*

Combine all ingredients. If you are freezing for later
use, make sure solids are covered with liquid from
corn and chestnuts.

Yields: 1 quart (can be made in larger quantities
               and frozen)
Preparation: 10 minutes

*"Jack suggests slicing the chestnuts by hand
instead of with a food processor. The difference in
texture is worth the extra elbow grease."*

—NOTES—

Doe-Al Country Cookin'

South Pasadena

You really can't compare Southern cooking with "soul food" at Doe-Al Country Cookin'. As owner Doretha Bacon explains, "The 'Southern' refers to the area, using Southern-grown vegetables put together in a Southern way. My version of 'soul food' is a recipe you can do anywhere. It's what a person feels. It stems from not usin' (written) recipes but cookin' from the inside. Just a dash of this and a dash of that...."

Mrs. Bacon's version of popular Southern dishes comes from her own experience. A native of St. Petersburg, she went to school in New York and then became a dietician for a large hospital and nursing home. When her husband was in the service, they traveled frequently and sampled food at restaurants everywhere, particularly in the South. Doretha was a pro at taking food backstage at theaters where her brothers, who were professional jazz musicians, performed.

She decided to enter the restaurant business because she loved sales and people contact. Doretha opened the first Doe-Al Country Kitchen in south St. Petersburg in 1969. Soon after, the name was changed to Doe-Al Country

Cookin'. Now two restaurants are operating; one in South Pasadena and another in north St. Petersburg.

Barbecue was the original specialty. In addition to the barbecue, the Doe-Al now features a family-style menu, with Southern Fried Chicken, Brunswick Stew, Cajun Rice, Black-Eyed Peas, and many other regional favorites. While the lunch menu is printed, the dinner menu is scribbled by hand, on a paper bag no less, to accommodate day-to-day changes. Corn Meal Muffins accompany most orders, or you can order extras. They're served piping hot, with a large dollop of butter on the side. It's tough to eat just one!

Doretha rarely slows down except for an annual vacation. During the holiday season, she maintains a hectic pace—from supervising the baking of 200 pies a week to adding finishing touches on newly made curtains.

Bring the family to enjoy a tasty home-cooked meal prepared with lots of warmth. Servings are as generous as the hospitality, and you'll get a wholesome lunch or dinner for less than you'd pay at fast food places. And don't forget to sample the king-size chocolate chip and oatmeal cookies. They're a find you won't forget.

Directions: There are two locations. Doe-Al Country Cookin' is at 1480 Pasadena Avenue South in St. Petersburg, From I-275 in St. Petersburg, turn west at the 22nd Avenue South exit. 22nd Avenue becomes Gulfport Boulevard, which you will follow along the Pasadena Golf Course until it intersects with Pasadena Avenue. Turn left to address; the Doe-Al is across the street from the Palms of Pasadena Hospital. Or, from U.S. 19 north or south, turn west at 22nd Avenue South and follow same directions.

Doe-Al Country Cookin's second location is at 1126 62nd Avenue North in St. Petersburg. From I-275 South, take the 54th Avenue North exit and head east to 16th Street. Turn north on 16th Street, then east onto 62nd Avenue to address.

While you're here: Less than a half-hour drive north is Heritage Park, in Largo. Several of Pinellas County's oldest buildings have been preserved in a wooded setting, and docents give tours explaining the lifestyle of families that settled the area in the 1800s. Some of the old-fashioned kitchen utensils in the "Seven Gables" house are particularly interesting.

Doe-Al Country Cookin'
South Pasadena and St. Petersburg

CAJUN RICE

(Prepare rice ahead)

6 C. hot cooked rice (Uncle Ben's or your favorite brand)
¼ C. bacon fat or vegetable oil
1 large onion, chopped
3 ribs celery, chopped
1 large green pepper, chopped
¼ C. parsley, chopped
1½ lbs. sausage meat, ground (sweet, if available)
½ lb. chicken gizzards, cooked, chopped
2 chicken bouillon cubes
¼ C. water
¼ t. red pepper
¼ t. garlic powder
½ t. powdered thyme
1 t. salt

Saute vegetables in bacon fat until clear, about 10 minutes. Add sausage meat and chicken gizzards to vegetables by "chopping in" the meat. Continue to cook. Dissolve bouillon cubes in water and add to meat and vegetables. Add seasonings and simmer 10 minutes. Add to hot, cooked rice. Toss or mix well and serve.

Serves: 8-10
Preparation: Rice—20-30 minutes. Mixture—
10 minutes (Mrs. Bacon recommends
chopping vegetables by hand rather
than in a food processor to preserve
the right texture)
Cooking: 20 minutes

*"By cooking the rice separate from the seasonings
mixture, the Cajun Rice dish retains a nice texture.
For best results, prepare the rice loose and dry,
rather than too moist or sticky. Be careful not to use
too much garlic, so it won't spoil quickly."*

—NOTES—

FRIED SUMMER SQUASH CASSEROLE

½   lb. bacon, chopped
4   lbs. yellow squash, sliced
2   large onions, sliced
½   t. salt
½   t. pepper
1   T. sugar

Fry bacon. Do not drain fat. Add sliced squash and onions and sauté. Mix seasonings together and sprinkle evenly over vegetables in pan. Continue to cook over medium heat, stirring constantly with a fork, about 15 to 18 minutes. Be careful not to break up vegetables so as to lose texture.

Serves: 6–8
Preparation: 10 minutes
Cooking: 15–18 minutes

"You won't have to add any liquid to this dish—the moisture comes from the squash and onions. A constant stirring will prevent pieces of the vegetables from sticking to the pan."

SOUTHERN FRIED CHICKEN

1   3-lb. fryer, cut in 6-8 pieces
    salt and coarse black pepper to taste
2   C. self-rising flour
1   C. buttermilk
    vegetable shortening

Season fryer with salt and coarse black pepper to taste. Let stand 3 hours. To bread, dip individual pieces first in flour, then in buttermilk, then back in flour. Fry covered, at 350°F., in heavy skillet with enough vegetable shortening to cover chicken pieces about half way up. Turn continually until done, about 15 to 20 minutes.

Serves: 4
Preparation: 10 minutes plus 3 hours to stand
Cooking: 20 minutes

"Covering the skillet creates steam and moisture to make this fried chicken just right. Thank you Mr. & Mrs. Bacon."

Ted Peters Famous Smoked Fish

South Pasadena

Smoked mullet and mackerel are the specialties at Ted Peters Famous Smoked Fish, yet it's been said that this local landmark could keep a rollicking business going just with hamburgers, even if the supply of fish were to dry up.

Ted had been in the smoked fish business and opened a fish house after World War II on St. Petersburg Beach. Not long after, he ran the Carolina Inn, formerly located next door to where the restaurant now stands. He asked his half-brother, Elry Lathrop, to manage the business during summer break. Elry was studying accounting in college and ran the show himself while Ted traveled around the country. They became partners and opened the restaurant in 1950, working together for about 10 years and then taking turns, every other month, for the next 14 years. Ted's now retired, and Elry and his son Mike are continuing the booming business.

Every year they smoke about 135,000 pounds of fish in the little smokehouse next to the restaurant building. They use native red oak to smoke and flavor the fish, which is placed on racks over a smouldering fire and cooked for four to six hours. The meat of the mullet has a nut-like flavor, and the natural oil between the skin and the meat helps to cook the fish slowly and keep it from drying out. Mackerel also has a high oil content but the skin is not so thick as with mullet. You can savor the smoked fish on the premises, at the shaded counter or at a picnic table or inside in the cozy dining room (the fireplace keeps it warm in the winter), or you can take some home. Don't be surprised if seagulls keep you company when you dine outside.

The menu is deliberately limited because, as Mike says, they want to maintain high quality with just a few familiar items. That keeps a good turnover rate at the tables, which means that many more people can enjoy the food.

One other specialty is potato salad, which arrived on the menu almost by accident. Mike's grandmother, Matilda Lathrop, had been handling the kitchen for years. One day, a large group made a reservation, and she simply refused, flat out, to make French fries for so many. Independent character that she was, she said, "I know what I'll do. I'll make German potato salad!" And she drew on what she had learned while living in Germany as a child. The resulting potato salad is now another famous menu item.

If you live in town, bring your out-of-state friends and relatives. If you *are* from out of town, you'll probably return home with *new* friends.

Directions: Ted Peters Famous Smoked Fish is at 1350 Pasadena Avenue South. From I-275 in St. Petersburg, turn west at the 22nd Avenue South exit. 22nd Avenue becomes Gulfport Boulevard, which you will follow along the Pasadena Golf Course (home of the Orange Blossom Classic) until it intersects with Pasadena Avenue. Turn left to address. Ted Peters is on the east side of the street. Or, from U.S. 19 north or south, turn west at 22nd Avenue South and follow same directions.

While you're here: Stay on Pasadena Avenue and cross the causeway to **St. Petersburg** *and* **Pass-a-Grille Beaches** *to soak in the sun. Take Pasadena Avenue back the other direction and visit the* **planetarium and observatory** *at* **St. Petersburg Junior College***. Several programs are offered from Labor Day through mid-May. Park Street, a scenic residential drive, is nearby.*

Ted Peters Smoked Fish
St. Petersburg

SMOKED FISH SPREAD

---

2   C. finely diced onion
1   C. finely diced celery
1½ C. sweet relish with pimiento
1¼ qts. Kraft Miracle Whip Salad Dressing
3½ qts. flaked smoked fish (boned), mullet
     preferred

Mix ingredients well. Chill. Best if served in
2 to 3 days.

Serves: a party
Preparation: 10 minutes

"It's so good you could eat a whole gallon yourself."

Hampton's

Daytona Beach

Tell somebody something often enough, and after a while they'll believe you, especially if it's true.

That's what happened to earn Hampton's the right to say on the menu, "World's Best Chicken." So many customers gave it that label that Joan and Jack Phillips decided to adopt it as their slogan in the 1970s. They've been delivering on that promise ever since, and today owners Gary and Barry Moore are continuing the tradition, serving excellent fried chicken.

Joan says it's not the recipe that's so special but the method of cooking. They use a high-pressure broaster that's so large it won't fit in the typical home pantry. It creates 350 pounds of pressure and requires quite a bit of know-how both to operate and to take apart and clean, Joan explains. Maybe a unit like a Wearever would work at home, something that seals the juices in, but it just wouldn't be the same as at Hampton's. . . .

At any rate, Jack was the restaurant's very first chicken cook. You can tell that chicken is the heart and soul of this restaurant not only from the food itself and the popularity of the take-out window, but also from the collection of chicken statues and memorabília. The oversize chicken near the front entrance was made just for them. They've even mounted it on a dune buggy to ride in Christmas parades on the beach.

If you want to know the secret of all those full-bodied flavors in Hampton's recipes, heed Joan's advice: save **everything.** Keep a big jar to fill up in the refrigerator, and save leftover vegetables for soup. When you cook meat, save the drippings and use them as a base for sauces and gravy. Call it "Ma's Kettle" and don't throw anything away. Throw in a healthy dose of Accent and very little salt. You'll get more mileage out of your food dollar for delicious casseroles and stews. (Be sure to boil the accumulated flavorings before re-use and to use them within just a few days.)

Good value is what's kept people coming back to "mama's house" year after year, says Joan. There are students from Embry Riddle Aeronautical University, race crew members, senior citizens, and municipal workers. Even patients who've been in the hospital seem to start their recovery diets here.

Hampton's is also known for its foot-long hot dogs, "like you grew up on." Don't be chicken. . .try one!

Directions: Hampton's is at 1116 Mason Avenue. From U.S. 92 (Volusia Avenue) heading east, turn north on Clyde Morris Boulevard, past the hospitals to Mason Avenue. Turn east on Mason to address, on the north side of the street.

166

While you're here: *Go for a ride on the Beach. ("Do not pass Go, do not collect $200. . . .") It's the key to what first made Daytona famous. Of course, if you're in town during any of the race weeks, you'll spend your time at the* **Daytona International Speedway,** *rubbing elbows with greats like Richard Petty and A.J. Foyt in local grub and beer centers. From a quiet, mellow spirit the rest of the year, these same spots take on a totally different character when thousands of students pour into town for Spring Break. Off-season visit the home of* **Mary McLeod Bethune,** *well-known black educator and founder of what eventually became Bethune-Cookman College. About a half-hour's ride north of Daytona Beach near Flagler Beach are the* **Bulow Plantation Ruins,** *once a magnificent and prosperous enterprise until its destruction in 1836 during the Second Seminole War.*

—NOTES—

MOIST CHICKEN LIVERS

---

1   lb. chicken livers, washed and patted dry (allow
    6-8 oz. per serving)
    oil for deep frying
    commercial breading mix or flour to which
    Accent has been added
2   medium onions, chopped
    gravy mix*
    butter

Dip livers in breading or flour and deep fry as if
preparing fried chicken. Set aside. Sauté onions in
some butter and stir into gravy mix. Pour mixture
over livers and let sit for 15 minutes. Next sauté
livers in butter or oil until warmed.

Serves: 2-4
Preparation: 10 minutes
Cooking: about 5 minutes each for frying and
           sautéing

*"Chicken livers cooked this way are tender and
delicious. Serve with rice or buttered pasta."*

*Available packaged in your local supermarket, or use your own.

BAKED BEANS

2 oz. liquid smoke
2 oz. vinegar
2 oz. Worcestershire sauce
1 lb. brown sugar
1 lb. light brown sugar
½ gallon catsup
leftover barbecue meat, chopped (or commercially prepared barbecue sauce with pork or beef added)
3 cans Showboat baked beans or your favorite brand

Combine liquid smoke, vinegar, Worcestershire, brown sugars, and catsup, and heat just to the boiling point. Stir occasionally to melt sugars and blend ingredients. Add leftover barbecue meat and baked beans. Stir frequently until mixture thickens. For an extra taste treat, dip fried chicken in sauce.

Serves: 8–10 as a main dish
Preparation: 5 minutes
Cooking: 10–15 minutes

"Adding the barbecue meat gives the beans a delicious flavor. Here's a good Sunday night supper recipe."

*Hampton's
Daytona Beach*

PICKLED BEETS

(Allow time to chill)

1   16-oz. can crinkle cut beets (straight cut beets
     may be substituted, but the crinkle type
     absorbs the flavor better)
⅓   C. sugar
3   T. vinegar

Drain juice from canned beets into a saucepan and
set beets aside. Add sugar and vinegar to juice and
bring to a boil. Add beets and bring to a boil again.
Let sit at room temperature, about 2 hours, to cool
down before chilling. Be careful not to overcook
beets as they will flake.

Yields: about 4 cups
Preparation: 5 minutes plus cooling and chilling
                    time
Cooking: about 10 minutes

*"The degree of pickling in this dish is just right. Or,
you can add sliced raw onions for a different flavor."*

LUCY'S BANANA PIE

2   C. water
1½   oz. dry milk (low-fat base)
1½   oz. cornstarch
½   C. sugar
2   eggs
½   t. vanilla
1½-2   bananas, sliced (depending on pie shell size)
1   pre-baked pie shell
           whipped cream or Cool Whip

Stir water, milk, and cornstarch in saucepan until
cornstarch is thoroughly mixed in. Bring to boil and
add remaining ingredients except fruit. Stir with wire
whisk until mixture thickens. Divide and fold into pie
shell. Add banana slices in layers. Chill. Add whipped
cream or Cool Whip and serve.

Yields: 1 pie
Preparation: 10-15 minutes plus 1 hour to chill

*"For variations, use ¾ C. coconut instead of or in
addition to bananas. For Peanut Butter Pie, cook
base thicker so that it doesn't become runny when
peanut butter is added. Sprinkle flour over ¾ C.
peanut butter in bowl. Knead with a fork into 1-inch
balls and add to base instead of bananas."*

Old Spanish Sugar Mill and Griddle House, DeLeon Springs, Florida

The Old Spanish Sugar Mill

DeLeon Springs

Without a doubt, the most unusual restaurant in all of Florida's state recreation areas is the Old Spanish Sugar Mill at DeLeon Springs. The park was privately operated until 1982, when the state purchased it, but the Schwarze family continues to operate the mill and the griddle house as they have since 1962.

What's so unusual is not only the mill itself but how the pancakes are prepared there. Inside the restaurant, long wooden tables have rectangular electric griddles sunken into their tops. *You* pour the batter (prepared from grains ground on the French buhr millstones) on the griddle yourself and fix them just the way you like!

Now what could be more "down home" than that? The nice thing is that you don't have to worry about cleaning up.

Patty Schwarze tells the mill's story. The original structure, built long before the Civil War, was a sugar mill. During that war it was used for corn that was shipped down the St. John's River. The mill burned down but was rebuilt. Later it became run-down again. Patty's father, a fifth-generation grist miller who had always loved old buildings, got together with the park owners and restored the mill himself.

Today's building looks like an old country store with a friendly, camp-like atmosphere. With the fresh-water spring and sloping lawn outside for sunning, it's the perfect day camp setting for the whole family. Even the peacocks get into the act. The males spread their brightly-hued feathers so often that the sight isn't a novelty but rather is an expected element of natural beauty.

In addition to the cook-'em-yourself pancakes, there's an assortment of other breakfast items, hot and cold sandwiches, salads, fruit, and cheese—everything you'd take with you if you were packing a picnic basket. But the specialty remains the selection of fresh, stone-ground flours for the pancakes and fresh-baked bread. These include whole wheat, rye, natural white, soya, sprouted wheat, and five-grain honey. It's a labor of love to make the flour. Even though the park closes down for the night and the restaurant closes with it, the mill stays busy, baking bread until the wee hours of the morning. It's a costly and time-consuming process, but it's a small price to pay for real, wholesome food.

Go on out and spend the day!

Directions: *From I-4 East or West, take U.S. 17-92 North, just north of Deltona, through DeLand and into DeLeon Springs. Stay on 17-92 and follow signs to the park.*

While you're here: *If the day at the park isn't enough, you can visit the* **Pioneer Settlement for the Creative Arts,** *a museum and winter crafts school in a pioneer homestead environment. It's located just off the intersection of 17-92 and SR 40. Be sure to visit the kitchen and see how jellied citrus candies are made. Then backtrack to DeLand and visit* **Stetson University,** *another Florida landmark, many of whose buildings date from the 19th century. Save time especially for the* **Rice Planetarium.**

GRANOLA CEREAL

4   lbs. rolled oats
½   lb. shredded coconut
½   lb. macro* flaked rye
½   lb. macro flaked wheat
½   lb. sunflower seeds
½   lb. millett
6   oz. sesame seeds
1   C. vegetable oil, preferably non-hydrogenated
1   C. honey
    cashews
    raisins
    dates

Mix grains and seeds. Combine oil and honey and add to dry mixture. Bake at 300°F. until brown, stirring frequently. Add any amount desired of cashews, raisins, and dates. Store in tightly covered containers.

Yields: a very large quantity! (20–30 large servings)
Preparation: 10 minutes
Cooking: depends on quantity

"Not only is this a delicious cereal, it's also a great snack!

*Available in health food stores

SOY GRITS FOR BALANCED PROTEIN BREAD

½ C. soybeans* per pound of dough or flour
   your favorite whole wheat bread recipe (such as
   Tassajara)

Toast soybeans to make grits for 10 minutes at
400 °F. Crack in a Vitamix or blender or handmill, a
few at a time. "Throw" cracked soybean chunks into
favorite whole wheat recipe and bake bread per usual
instructions.

Yields: 1 loaf
Preparation: 15 minutes plus bread recipe
Cooking: depends on your recipe

*"This bread has a nutty texture and contains lots of
protein for a good, nutritious treat."*

*Available in health food stores

CARAWAY BAKED POTATOES

5-6 baking potatoes, scrubbed
2   C. rye flour
    water
1   C. unbleached white flour
2-3 T. ground caraway

Bake the potatoes for 10 minutes in a 350°F. oven and then cool completely. Mix enough water into the flours and caraway to make a thick dough. Knead for a few minutes if necessary. Wrap each potato in a layer of dough and seal edges with water. Bake in a 350°F. oven (directly on the oven rack) for 45 to 60 minutes. Serve with casing on and butter on the side.

Serves: 5-6
Preparation: 5-10 minutes
Cooking: 45-60 minutes

"We found that the preliminary baking of the potatoes before wrapping in dough ensured that both the potato and dough would be cooked at the same time."

Oviedo Inn

Oviedo

A short ride away from Orlando's bustling tourist industry and burgeoning electronics firms, there's a quiet little haven where it's like going to Grandma's to spend a day in the country.

Just northeast of Orlando is the small town of Oviedo, where Tom and Kathleen Estes run their lovely Oviedo Inn. Appearing seemingly out in the middle of nowhere, this rustic building looks like a nice, large home.

It's just as attractive inside as outside, with fresh flowers dotting wooden tables covered with print tablecloths. There's a great stone fireplace and real wood paneling. Much of this detail and the overall design are a result of Tom's own craftsmanship. Even though you probably won't know the people in the pictures, it's fun to look at the photos on the walls from Oviedo High School in the 1930s.

The photos on the menu go back to the turn of the century, showing the Oviedo area as it used to be. "Editorial" comments on the menu give clues about each dish, for example, specials that are "ready when you are," and desserts "to reward you just for waking up today." If you have a country-size appetite, you'll more than get your fill.

Desserts are listed *first* on the menu. That's to tip you off that they're delicious enough to warrant planning the rest of your meal to leave room for them at the end. Tortes, cobblers, fruit meringues, bread puddings, ice cream pies. . . well, you get the idea.

The chef and all of the cooking staff have had outstanding culinary experience and training, which show on the menu and in the preparation. One unusual entree is *Boneless Barbecue Beef Ribs,* recommended "for the sauce or because folks don't have to fight the ribs to get at all that good beef."

Homemade soups, sauces, salad dressing, cinnamon rolls. . . they're all fresh. Mmmm!

Directions: *The Oviedo Inn is on SR 426 (Aloma Avenue). From I-4 in Orlando, take the Colonial Drive exit east to SR 436 (Semoran Boulevard) or the East-West Expressway (toll) to the same road. Follow 436 north and turn east on SR 426, about a 15-minute ride to the Inn, depending on traffic. You can also reach 426 from I-4 north by taking the SR 436 exit east and following it south, beyond Red Bug and Howell Branch Roads, until it intersects with 426.*

While you're here: *The Orlando area is known for the world's best theme parks. On the quieter side, not far from Oviedo, is* **Winter Park,** *a well-established, older community northwest of the city. Princely oak trees line its main shopping street,* **Park Avenue,** *and it's home to* **Rollins College,** *the state's oldest private school. A scenic boat cruise offers glimpses of old and not-so-old mansions built along the town's numerous and delightful lakes. The* **Morse Art Gallery,** *with stained glass work by Louis B. Tiffany, is only one of the many art centers in the area.*

NEW ENGLAND CORN CHOWDER

2   oz. bacon
½   cup diced onions
½   oz. flour
8   oz. chicken stock
1   cup creamed corn
3   small potatoes, diced and cooked until just
    tender
½   pint whole milk, heated
½   cup light cream, heated
    salt, white pepper, and garlic powder to taste

Chop or grind bacon. Cook until bacon starts to render fat. Add onions and sauté until tender. Add flour and mix well. Cook without browning, 3 to 4 minutes. Slowly add chicken stock, stirring until smooth. Add corn, potatoes, milk, cream, and seasonings. Heat gently.

Serves: 5–6
Preparation: 10 minutes
Cooking: 15 minutes

"This recipe may come from New England, but try it with fresh Florida corn from Zellwood Station!"

Oviedo Inn
Oviedo

BAKED HAM AND FRUIT SAUCE

1   ham, fully cooked (6–8 oz. per serving)
½   cup honey
    ground cloves to taste
2   cans fruit cocktail
1   can water
1   T. cinnamon
1   t. cloves
5   oz. brown sugar
2   T. apple cider vinegar
    cornstarch
1–2 drops red food coloring (optional)

Make mixture of honey and ground cloves. Score
ham with a sharp knife, making cuts a half-inch apart.
Smear honey mixture on ham and bake for one hour
at 350°F.

FRUIT SAUCE
Drain fruit cocktail juice into a pot and save fruit for
use later. Add one can of water to fruit juice and
bring to a boil. Add remaining ingredients except
cornstarch and food coloring and return to a boil.
Dissolve enough cornstarch in water to add to juice
to thicken it. Simmer 3 to 4 minutes. When mixture is
thickened to desired consistency, add fruit cocktail.
Return to boil. Add food coloring if desired. Serve
fruit sauce with ham.

Serves: 6–10 depending on size of ham
Preparation: ham—5–10 minutes
               sauce—10 minutes
Cooking: ham—1 hour
           sauce—10 minutes

*"The fruit cocktail can be substituted with canned
apricots or peaches but omit the cloves."*

181

APPLESAUCE

---

10   large cooking apples
1   C. water
1   C. sugar
2   t. nutmeg
1   t. cinnamon

Wash, pare and quarter apples. Remove core. Place apples in saucepan with water. Cook over medium heat, covered, until tender, about 15–20 minutes. Stir in sugar, nutmeg, and cinnamon. Reduce heat and cook 5 minutes more. Serve hot or cold (chill about 1 hour).

Serves: 8
Preparation: 10 minutes
Cooking: 20–25 minutes (plus time to chill if served
           cold)

"This recipe reverses the cinnamon-nutmeg ratio, which makes it a spicy sauce. Serve as a side dish."

BREAD PUDDING

½ stick butter or margarine
10 slices white bread
1½ qts. coffee cream, divided
10 eggs
2 C. sugar
    pinch salt
1 t. vanilla
    nutmeg and cinnamon to taste
    raisins (optional)

Melt butter in 9 x 13 x 2-inch pan and set aside. Break up bread and place in large bowl. Pour 1 qt. of cream over bread and set aside. Break eggs into mixing bowl and add sugar. Beat until eggs are foamy and sugar is mixed in. Add salt and vanilla. Continue to beat while adding remaining ½ qt. of cream. Pour into bowl with bread-and-cream mixture. Stir lightly with large spoon. Pour into pan with melted butter. Sprinkle nutmeg and cinnamon on top. Add raisins if desired. Place in larger pan with ¼-inch deep water. Bake in 350°F. oven 1 hour, or until knife inserted in center comes out clean. Serve warm or cold, with lemon sauce (see page 184) and whipped cream or heavy cream.

Serves: 12
Preparation: 15 minutes
Cooking: 1 hour

"This is more of a custard than a pudding. It is absolutely delicious warm or cold, sauced or not."

Oviedo Inn
Oviedo

LEMON SAUCE

---

2   T. cornstarch
1   C. sugar
½   t. salt
2   C. water
4   T. lemon juice
2   egg yolks, beaten
2   T. butter, melted

Mix cornstarch, sugar, and salt. Add water and stir until smooth. Cook over medium heat until mixture is clear and thickened, about 8–10 minutes. Add lemon juice and cook 1 minute. Remove from heat. Pour in beaten egg yolks and stir in melted butter. Mix thoroughly. Serve slightly warm.

Yields: about 3 cups
Preparation: 2 minutes
Cooking: 10 minutes

"Serve over Bread Pudding (page 183). Reduce the amount of sugar if you prefer a sauce that is more tart."

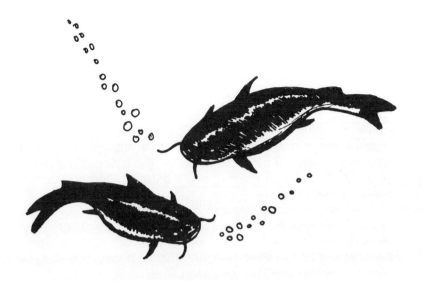

The Catfish Place

St. Cloud

If you've ever gotten tired of picking bones out of what was supposed to be filleted fish, or if you haven't quite adapted to eating the bones as well as the meat on fingerling catfish, try Steve and Judy Johnson's Catfish Place.

The fish are brought in, skinned, cleaned, washed, fillets removed from the backbone and cut in thin strips. They're lightly rolled in corn meal and cooked evenly throughout. They hardly even taste "fishy," and you'll almost never find a bone. Of course, you can order fingerlings here, too, and eat the bones if you wish. But the strips are a specialty that you're not likely to find elsewhere.

To keep a constant supply of outstanding catfish on hand, Steve buys from about two dozen different commercial fishermen, with deliveries all week long. He keeps the fresh fish in a large walk-in freezer, with ice placed at the bottom of big white plastic tubs with holes for draining. The fish are placed on *top* of the ice. The air from the walk-in keeps the fish cold on top, and it stays fresh longer.

Steve insists that the breading be done at the last minute just before cooking to insure maximum lightness and freshness. He's the only one who knows the exact 10 ingredients in his breading mix, which he sprinkles over damp fish strips placed in a stainless steel pan. Then he adds just enough water to wet the pan but not so much as to wash off the meal. Next, he rolls the fish well in more meal, picking up each piece and letting the meal fall off except for a fine coating. Finally, he drops the strips into a deep fat fryer for about three minutes, at 350°F. At home, though, if you add too many pieces of cold fish to the oil, the frying oil temperature may be lowered too much. It's better to drop only a few pieces in at a time.

The Catfish Place has a fish market adjacent to the restaurant and sells both fish and some 5,000 pounds of cole slaw a week to countless other restaurants around the state. Another specialty served here is turtle, with the bone *and* the fat removed for a milder taste than usual.

Don't get carried away and try to catch the fish in the 400-gallon salt-water aquarium dividing the restaurant section from the oyster bar. But do dig in to a plate of catfish. This is the kind of place where you "chat and chew."

Directions: *The Catfish Place is at the corner of U.S. 192 (13th Street) and Alabama Avenue. U.S. 192 is St. Cloud's "main drag," about 19 miles east of the I-4 exit for* **Walt Disney World.**

While you're here: *The* **Reptile World Serpentarium** *just east of St. Cloud and the* **Gatorland Zoo** *in Kissimmee should provide you with your fill of viewing snakes, turtles, alligators, and crocodiles. If you're more domestically inclined and are interested in home economics, tour the* **Tupperware International Headquarters** *and museum of food containers, two miles north of Kissimmee.*

CATFISH

---

4   catfish fillets, cut in 2-3-inch strips
    salt and pepper to taste
    Accent (same amount as salt)
    dash paprika
1   cup corn meal, stone ground
    oil for frying

Lightly season corn meal with salt, pepper and
Accent. Add a little paprika for coloring. Dip catfish
strips in meal mixture and deep fry until golden
brown. Fish gets cooked evenly throughout.

Serves: 2-4
Preparation: 10 minutes
Cooking: 5 to 10 minutes

*"Chef Steve Johnson insists on using only fresh,
stone-ground corn meal made by old-time Georgia
Crackers who live in the woods near Atlanta. Their
meal looks like real fine face powder, he says, and is
also good for making grits."*

HUSHPUPPIES

¾ lbs. sugar
¼ C. baking powder
¾ t. salt
¾ t. pepper
¾ t. garlic salt
1⅛ lbs. onion, diced
2 eggs
10 oz. milk
1¼ lbs. flour
1¼ lbs. corn meal

Mix sugar, baking powder, salt, pepper, and garlic salt. Blend onions, eggs, and milk in blender until onions have a texture like a milkshake, not too thin, and add to dry mixture until moist. Let sit until mixture bubbles, about 3 to 5 minutes. Meanwhile, mix flour and corn meal in a separate bowl and gradually add to liquid mixture. The resulting batter should be thick, like a cookie dough. If it is too watery, add more corn meal and flour; if it is too thick, add more milk. Deep fat fry by the half-teaspoonful in very hot oil, 375°F. By frying only a few at a time, hushpuppies will cook quickly and have a light, airy texture.

Yields: about 250 (great for a large party)
Preparation: 15 minutes
Cooking: depends upon quantity

"The batter keeps well in the refrigerator, as long as six weeks. The original recipe made 2,000 hushpuppies—we cut the recipe down a bit...."

COLE SLAW

2½ lbs. cabbage
1   carrot, grated
1   C. sweet salad dressing (Piknik, if available.
       Do *not* use mayonnaise.)
¾   C. sugar
       pinch salt
       pinch garlic salt
       pinch black pepper
⅓   t. red wine vinegar
       dash onion, chopped fine

Chop off bottom of cabbage, cut in quarters, and remove core. Grate. Mix by hand in large bowl with other ingredients. Chill and serve.

Serves: 8–10
Preparation: 10 minutes

"The very light use of seasonings and just a little bit of onion keeps this slaw from having an overpowering taste. It's popular with everyone."

Suncrest Restaurant

Melbourne

The way Elizabeth Ford (Betty, to all of her guests) runs her Suncrest Restaurant is just the way you like to see a small business managed. The restaurant is like a 1950s-era coffee shop, and the servings are gigantic. If you have a smaller appetite, order a half portion instead.

Lunch specials are planned for quick service. Not everything appears on the printed menu, so you'll frequently hear customers asking Betty, "What's for dinner, dear?" just like at home. And with four of her six children working there with her, it may as well be home.

Betty entered the restaurant business after being a cook in New York City and catering Viennese Tables. These were elaborate affairs, flaming dessert smorgasbords rolled out on tiered tables at fancy weddings and similar events. After vacationing in Florida and loving it, she eventually decided to move here. It was a natural for her, when she bought the Suncrest, to continue the original owner's tradition of delicious pies and home cooking.

We'd be remiss if we didn't pass on to you some of Betty's most successful cooking hints. For one thing, except for home fries and french fries, she uses very little grease for cooking, preferring to sauté and steam foods instead. She'll use water and only a little oil for salmon patties, for example, spraying her pans with Pam. Her gravy is made from a grease-free broth rather than a commercial mix. She puts leftovers to good use: after cooking 25 to 30 turkeys a week, she uses every part, in soup, salad, and croquettes. Homemade soups and clam or shrimp bisque are so thick "you can eat them with a fork." Only fresh fruits and vegetables ever appear on her salad plates.

Small wonder, then, that some of her customers eat literally *all* of their meals here!

About those large portions, now. Go in with a bear-size appetite for a mammoth blueberry muffin that must be four times the size of the average muffin, served with fresh honey from a nearby honey bee farm. Or when you order a "Super Suncrester," be prepared for a two-hand, five-napkin hamburger loaded with melted cheese, a pile of shaved ham, and a barbecue-like sauce. It's addictive!

Good news for diabetics, too. Betty makes a dietetic apple pie using water-packed apple slices and no saccharin or sugar.

Her greatest reward? Compliments from her guests. You'll add yours, too.

Directions: The Suncrest is at 914 New Haven Avenue (U.S. 192). The restaurant is on the north side of the street, approximately two miles west of the intersection of 192 with U.S. 1.

While you're here: If you're anywhere near the Space Coast when there's a launch planned, call for schedule information. The toll-free number is in the phone book. The **Kennedy Space Center** *tours at Cape Canaveral are dramatic memorials to modern history, not to be missed. About a half-hour drive in the opposite direction, south on A1A, is the* **McLarty State Museum** *at Sebastian Inlet, with displays of the hurricane wreck of two large Spanish treasure fleets in 1715.*

BEEF PINWHEELS

1   package Jiffy biscuit mix
    milk
    leftover pot roast or beef, sliced or diced
      (allow 6–8 oz. per serving)
    granulated garlic
    chopped parsley
    salt and pepper
    egg yolk, beaten
    gravy (homemade or commercial)

Follow the directions on the mix to make the batter BUT replace the water with milk. Knead for a few minutes. Divide dough in half and roll out so that it is quite thin. Use a rolling cutter or sharp knife and cut out strips approximately 3 by 5 inches. Place meat in a strip up the middle of each strip of dough. Sprinkle with garlic, parsley, salt (if needed), and pepper. Roll up and place seam side down in a pan that has been sprayed with Pam or Mazola No-stick. Brush each pinwheel with beaten egg yolk. Bake according to Jiffy package directions if using a conventional oven or 300°F. in a convection oven for 15 to 20 minutes. When done, slice each pinwheel on the diagonal and serve covered with gravy.

Serves: 4
Preparation: 15 minutes
Cooking: 10–20 minutes, depending upon oven used

"A good solution to the 'what-to-do-with-leftovers' problem."

RICE-BROCCOLI-CHEESE CASSEROLE

---

1   **box Minute Rice**
½   **No. 10 can Cheddar cheese sauce**
2   **13-oz. cans evaporated milk**
½   **lb. margarine or butter**
2   **large boxes frozen whole broccoli, defrosted**
     salt and pepper to taste
     grated cheese

Make Minute Rice. Pour cheese sauce over rice and add milk and margarine. Place broccoli on bottom of baking pan and pour rice mixture over top. Add salt and pepper to taste. Bake until casserole starts to bubble, about 15–20 minutes at 300°F. in a convection oven. Serve with a spatula, turning over so that broccoli is on top. Sprinkle with grated cheese.

Serves: 8–10
Preparation: 5–10 minutes
Cooking: 15–20 minutes in convection oven
            about 35 minutes in regular oven

"For variations, try ham, scalloped potatoes, or corn in addition to or instead of broccoli."

PEANUT BUTTER PIE

---

1   C. heavy cream
2   C. commercial liquid topping such as Rich's
2   boxes Jello instant Vanilla Pudding
4   heaping T. peanut butter
½   C. crushed nuts
1   baked pie shell
    chocolate fudge topping
    whipped cream for topping
    crushed nuts for garnish

Combine heavy cream, liquid whipped topping, and pudding. Whip until thick, fluffy, and completely blended. Add peanut butter and nuts. Fold into pie shell. Optional: swirl chocolate fudge topping through filling with a knife by dribbling over top and blending it in like a marble cake. Decorate with whipped cream or topping (topping will hold up better) and sprinkle with crushed nuts. Chill. Keep in refrigerator until ready to serve.

Serves: 6
Preparation: 10 minutes plus time to chill

"Peanut butter's not just for sandwiches anymore!"

Ye Tower Lunch

Lantana

A landmark in Lantana—hometown for *The National En-quirer*—is Ye Tower Lunch, a restaurant noted both for its tower and for being Palm Beach County's oldest business under the same ownership.

Actually, the tower isn't what it used to be. Paul Dunbar and his brother had purchased what was once a 55-foot-tall lookout platform used for prospective landowners during Florida's boom days. They converted it into a restaurant to cater to the then-small town. In just a few years, the town grew rapidly, with real estate development taking off and highway construction at the front door. Ye Tower Lunch became part of everyone's social life, the place to go after high school dances or for special events in the community.

But the killer hurricane of 1928, the same one that caused Lake Okeechobee to overflow and wipe out the population of several small towns, knocked down the 55-foot structure, and the tower that stands today is only a five-foot memorial.

Other than the smaller tower, the restaurant hasn't changed much in more than half a century. Well, there's been some rebuilding. . .when cars have driven through the front wall because there's almost no setback from the road, thanks to a provision in the deed that was grandfathered in and which kept the city from relocating the building. But the fixtures inside are original, even down to some of the glass and tableware. And if the soda fountain itself doesn't bring back memories, try sipping one of Paul's old-fashioned chocolate malts. The sandwiches and cheeseburgers are all the same as what he introduced to the area decades ago.

You'll get more than your fill of local history here. Paul was mayor of Lantana for nine years, served in other elected posts, and became a noted photographer whose photos chronicle the town's early growth. As a result of his efforts, a 3,000-foot strip along the beach will always be publicly owned, a kind of haven in contrast with miles of development elsewhere.

Ye Tower Lunch has become an institution in this small Florida town on the Gold Coast. To find home-style cooking at good prices makes it an unusual discovery well worth singling out.

Directions: Ye Tower Lunch is at 916 South Dixie Highway (U.S. 1). From I-95, take the Hypoluxo Road exit east to U.S. 1. Turn north on U.S. 1 for five blocks to address. Or, take the Lantana Road exit east to U.S. 1 and turn south for nine blocks. Ye Tower Lunch is on the east side of the street.

While you're here: One town north of Lantana is **Lake Worth**, *whose lakeshore lots were given away in the 1900s to those who purchased tracts of truck and fruit land elsewhere in town. Today, fresh-water fishing is popular at* **Lake Osborne**, *and salt-water fishing is the attraction from one of Florida's longest municipally-owned Atlantic Ocean piers. In Palm Beach see* **Worth Avenue**, *with its exclusive shops, and the* **Henry Morrison Flagler Museum**, *formerly the home of the big-time developer for whom it is named. The house cost $4-million to complete in 1902. Flagler's restored private railroad car is also on the grounds.*

*Ye Tower Lunch
Lantana*

PAUL DUNBAR'S CREAM PIES BASIC RECIPE

2　3-1/8-oz. boxes Jello Pudding Mix (not instant)
2　T. cornstarch
1　qt. milk
1　10-inch baked pie shell
　　whipped cream

Prepare 10-inch pie shell with your favorite recipe. In 2-quart saucepan add pudding mix, cornstarch, and milk. Cook over medium heat, stirring constantly for about 7 minutes or until boiling. *Do not overcook.* Cool to room temperature, then refrigerate until ready to use. After cooling, stir pudding and pour into pie shell. Top with whipped cream.

FOR CHOCOLATE PIE:
Follow same basic recipe using vanilla pudding mix, but add two 1-ounce squares of Baker's Semi-sweet Chocolate before cooking pudding. As it cooks, the chocolate melts and makes a richer chocolate pudding.

FOR BANANA PIE:
Follow same basic recipe using vanilla pudding mix. Cook and cool. Line bottom of pie shell with sliced bananas before pouring pudding into it.

FOR COCONUT PIE:
Follow same basic recipe using vanilla pudding mix. Cook and cool. Add 1 cup of Baker's Shredded Coconut to pudding, stir well, then pour into pie shell. Top with whipped cream and sprinkle with additional coconut.

FOR BUTTERSCOTCH PIE:
Follow same basic recipe using butterscotch pudding mix.

Yields:　1 pie each recipe
Preparation:　about 10 minutes plus time to chill

"This is a quick dessert if you have pre-baked pie shells on hand."

La Esquina de Tejas, Miami, Florida

To Wilfredo & Juan
With appreciation
& Very Best Regards
Ronald Reagan

La Esquina De Tejas

Miami

Until recently, La Esquina de Tejas was one among many Cuban restaurants in Miami's Little Havana district, simply going about business in the usual way. Since 1967, the popular corner restaurant, decked with ham hocks hanging in the windows, has been known for its sandwiches and good, standard Cuban fare. Specials are varied throughout the week, dishes like *Fricasé de Pollo* (roasted or stewed chicken), *Picadillo* (a ground beef and tomato sauce dish, *Sopa de Pescado* (fish soup) and similar items.

On Cuban Independence Day in May, 1983, the regular menu at La Esquina de Tejas became famous. President Reagan came to town and stopped in for lunch. He was warmly greeted by 204 diners, all of whom were there by special invitation of the owners.

One guest said, "I'm glad the President knows a good restaurant when he sees one."

Actually, the apparent spontaneity of the occasion was carefully planned. When co-owners Juan Vento and Wilfredo Chamizo received word of the impending visit, they quietly began to invite some of their "regulars," each of whom had

199

to be approved by security. The President's personal steward passed inspection on the kitchen and the menu, which was selected because there's a well-known restaurant by the same name in Cuba and because it offers typical Cuban food. Vento made no changes in the menu for the occasion, and what the president would eat was not determined in advance. But earlier in the day, the chef and his staff had prepared 50 pound of *moros* (black beans and rice), 120 *plátanos* (plantains, similar to bananas), 40 *pollos* (chickens), and 600 servings of *flan* (custard) for the rest of the week.

And President Reagan then enjoyed the No. 1 special of the day, *Pollo Asado, Moros y Plátanos*, accompanied by a miniature cup of strong-flavored Cuban coffee.

Vento has since placed in safe-keeping the table and chair where the President sat, and the table service that he used. Otherwise, everything is staying the same—the menu, the cheerful western-style decor with its wrought-iron sections along the counter, red brick tile floor, bright red accents and white tablecloths, and wood paneling in one of the dining rooms.

And you'll find, too, that the same hospitality and good wishes extended to the President are also offered to everyday guests. The name may say "Texas Corner" in translation, but it's *"Famous Florida!"* now.

Directions: La Esquina de Tejas is at 101 SW 12th Avenue. From U.S. 1 (Biscayne Boulevard) downtown, turn west on 1st Street NE, going under the North-South Expressway, after which 1st Street merges with Flagler. Turn left on 12th Avenue to address; La Esquina de Tejas is on the east side of the street.

While you're here: *Miami and Miami Beach are full of exciting sights and things to do. The* **Miami Herald** *newspaper building gives tours and is considered one of the most beautiful newspaper plants in the country. The* **Miami Seaquarium** *and* **Planet Ocean,** *both reached from Rickenbacker Causeway, are entertaining, educational centers for marine life and oceanography. By all means save time for shopping and soaking up the sunshine!*

POLLO ASADO (BAKED CHICKEN)

3   chickens cut into quarters
2   t. salt
2   garlic cloves
5   bitter oranges, squeezed (or equal parts of
     orange and lime juice)

Wash chicken and pat dry. Sprinkle with 1 teaspoon salt and pat in gently. Place chicken in one layer in a large pan and bake in a 400°F. oven for 1 hour. Remove and baste with a mixture of juice, garlic and salt. Return to the oven for another 30 minutes.

Serves: 4–6
Preparation: 15 minutes
Cooking: 90 minutes

"When making the basting mixture, combine the ingredients in a jar and shake well. If you are on a low sodium diet, the salt can be omitted."

La Esquina De Tejas
Miami

MOROS (MIXED BLACK BEANS)

12 oz. dry black beans
2 liters plus 6 oz. water
3 oz. olive oil
1 medium green pepper, minced
1 medium onion, minced
5 oz. (about 10 strips) bacon, diced
2 T. salt
3 T. garlic powder
1 T. Accent
1 T. cumin powder
6 laurel or bay leaves
1 t. oregano
1 lb. 4 oz. uncooked rice

Wash beans well. Place in a pressure cooker with water and cook for 25–30 minutes until the beans are soft. The beans and water can also be cooked in a covered pot for 1½–2 hours. Remove from heat. Heat olive oil in a medium skillet and sauté green pepper, onion and bacon until vegetables are golden. Stir into beans along with the remainder of ingredients except rice. Bring to a boil and add rice. Stir and cook for 5 minutes. Cover skillet (or a casserole dish) and bake in a 350°F. oven for 30 minutes. Stir well and cook for an additional 10 minutes.

Serves: 6
Preparation: 20 minutes
Cooking: about 40 minutes plus time to cook the beans

"This dish may remind you of Hoppingjohn (see recipe page 66). Both are excellent."

PLÁTANOS MADUROS (FRIED SWEET BANANAS)

---

4   very ripe* bananas, peeled and cut into 1-inch
     slices
1   cup vegetable or olive oil

Heat the oil in a skillet until it is about 350°F. Fry
bananas until both sides are golden.

Serves: 4
Preparation: 5 minutes
Cooking: until golden

*"If you are going to use the bananas as a dessert, fry
in vegetable oil and sprinkle with a little powdered
sugar. Use olive oil if the bananas are going to be a
side dish. Plantains are similar to bananas and are
commonly served in Spanish and Cuban restaurants."*

*The secret lies in the bananas' ripeness.

La Esquina De Tejas
Miami

FLAN (CARAMEL CUSTARD)

1   C. sugar
1   C. water plus 2 oz.
1   oz. Anisette
1   oz. cinnamon sticks (don't use powdered
     cinnamon)
6   large egg yolks
6   oz. condensed milk
6   oz. evaporated milk
6   oz. whole milk
⅛   t. salt
6   oz. grated coconut

Cook sugar and 2 oz. of water over high heat, stirring constantly. Pour resulting caramel into 6 molds or custard cups and cool. (As you pour, swirl caramel around so that it coats sides and bottom of molds.) Boil together for 10 minutes: the 1 cup water, Anisette and cinnamon sticks. Remove cinnamon sticks. Cool slightly. Stir in all eggs, milks, salt, and coconut. Mix until smooth and creamy. Pour into molds that have been coated with caramel. Place molds in a baking pan and fill with hot water to come half way up sides of molds. Bake in a 300°F. oven for 45 minutes or until a toothpick inserted into middle of flan comes out clean.

Serves: 6
Preparation: 15 minutes
Cooking: 45 minutes

"Flan can be served chilled, at room temperature, or slightly warm. This one's great."

Malaga

Miami

Between West Flagler Street and SW Eighth Street (U.S. 41) in Miami, just north of Coral Gables, pulses another "country," Little Havana, *la capital del exilio cubano*. All up and down the main streets and the side alleys, the area has become like Cuba transplanted, especially during the past 20 years or so. The cultural life of the country has been imported and adapted to mingle with American customs. Shops of all kinds, professional offices, bakeries and produce stands resound with a mixture of Cuban, Spanish and Mexican dialects. The eateries range from large, colorful *bodega*-style structures (a *bodega* can be either a grocery store or a wine cellar), to tiny sandwich shops where you almost never hear a word of English.

One unprepossessing establishment whose exterior hardly even hints at the feast within is Malaga, a frequent top choice among many restaurant reviewers. Its informal yet elegant *ambiente* combined with its generous servings of traditional Latin fare at surprisingly low prices have anchored its place as a "Calle Ocho" (Eighth Street neighborhood) restaurant.

After coming to the United States, owners José and Teresa Fernández operated an award-winning restaurant for some time in Chicago. They relocated to Miami, specifically to Little Havana, precisely because it was so much like Cuba. In 1975 they purchased the Malaga. Teresa's mother also moved here with them and helps them run the restaurant.

Malaga, named for a Spanish city that was Picasso's birthplace, exudes warmth with bright red tablecloths, dark wood rafters, and Spanish plates and works of art on the walls. The restaurant entrance is actually an open area between these rooms and leads directly into a delightful courtyard with brick tiles and fruit trees. Beyond the courtyard is another building with several private dining rooms, each outfitted with its own matched set of tableware. It's hard to believe the setting is so gracious and refined as the prices are so reasonable.

The service is appropriately warm, with hospitality the key whether you speak English or Spanish. Cuban, Spanish, and Mexican dishes are popular, as is the seafood. And their specialties such as roast chicken and a choice preparation of red snapper can be appreciated in any language.

Welcome—*bienvenido*!

Directions: Malaga is at 740 SW Eighth Street (U.S. 41, Tamiami Trail). Eighth Street is one-way heading east, so from I-95, when you take the exit ramp for U.S. 41, you will drive west on Seventh Street, turn left on Eighth Avenue, and left again onto Eighth Street to address.

*While you're here: For information on Hispanic festivals held throughout the year, call the Latin Chamber of Commerce or the Little Havana Tourist Authority (see your phone book or call Directory Assistance). Not far from Little Havana is **Vizcaya**, virtually a palace that was once the estate of early 20th-century industrialist James Deering, developer of modern agricultural machinery. Home of the **Dade County Art Museum**, Vizcaya is an Italian-style palazzo, with formal gardens, that became a model for structures later built in Miami and Coral Gables.*

PICADILLO (LATIN VERSION OF SLOPPY JOES)

1 onion, chopped
1 large chili pepper, chopped (remove seeds first)
2 cloves garlic, crushed
   oil for sautéing
1 lb. ground beef
1 t. salt
1 t. chopped pimiento
½ C. capers, drained, rinsed, and crushed
½ C. tomato sauce
¼ C. dry white wine
   raisins (optional)

Sauté onion, chili pepper, and garlic until onion
starts to brown. Add ground beef. When beef begins
to brown, add the rest of the ingredients. Stir well.
Cover and simmer 20 minutes. Drain excess juice
before serving.

Serves: 6
Preparation: 5-10 minutes
Cooking: 25 minutes

*"Be sure to wear rubber gloves when removing the
seeds of any hot pepper. If you forget and rub your
eyes within the next few hours, you will remember
the next time! Serve with rice and/or beans or on
buns."*

CARNE ASADA MECHADA
(POT ROAST OR ROAST BEEF, CUBAN STYLE)

(Allow time to marinate)

3	lbs. beef (pot roast or roast beef)
3	oz. bacon or ham, minced
2	carrots, minced
	garlic to taste, crushed
½	small jar pimiento
1	t. oregano
1	t. meat tenderizer
2	bay leaves
2	T. lemon juice
2	large onions, sliced
½	C. oil
1	C. dry red wine

Make deep slashes across the fat of the beef in a diamond pattern (as if scoring a ham). Mix finely minced ham or bacon and carrots together and stuff into cuts. Season meat with garlic, pimiento, oregano, meat tenderizer, bay leaf and lemon juice. Cover with onion rings and refrigerate for at least 6 hours. Drain meat (reserve marinade), pat dry, and brown in hot oil. Add wine and all of the marinade ingredients plus salt to taste. Cover tightly and cook over a low heat until done. Add additional wine and water as necessary to prevent meat from sticking to pan. Do not overcook. Defat gravy and taste for seasonings. Serve sliced with some of the marinade ingredients on top.

Serves: 4-6
Preparation: 10 minutes plus time for marinating
Cooking: 2-3 hours

"This goes well with black beans and/or rice, or boiled potatoes."

208

POLLO FRITO (FRIED CHICKEN)

1   2-lb. frying chicken
1   clove garlic, crushed
1   t. oregano
1   sour orange or 2 lemons, sliced
1   large onion, sliced into rings
¼   C. shortening or oil for frying
    salt to taste
¼   jar pimiento or ½ red pepper, chopped

Cut chicken in quarters. Wash, pat dry, and marinate
in crushed garlic, oregano, and lemon or orange
slices. Cover with onion rings and refrigerate. Sauté
chicken pieces on both sides in hot oil. When golden
brown, sprinkle lightly with salt and pimiento. Add
marinade ingredients. Cook over low heat, covered
tightly, for 25 minutes.

Serves: 4
Preparation: 15–20 minutes plus time to marinate
Cooking: 25 minutes

*"This is not fried chicken as such. It's more of a
flavorful chicken stew. Marinate as long as possible."*

SHRIMP IN GARLIC SAUCE, MALAGA-STYLE

2   lbs. jumbo shrimp
2   large onions
3   cloves fresh garlic or to taste
1   small bunch parsley, chopped
½   C. olive oil
1   t. salt
1   t. pepper
1   C. dry wine Chablis
1   T. finely grated cheese, such as Parmesan
3   T. butter
1   can green peas
1   can pimiento strips
      rice

Rinse shrimp well, peel shells, and devein. Be careful not to cut off tail. Mash garlic and chop onions thoroughly. Mix in blender: parsley, oil, salt and pepper, wine, cheese, butter, garlic, and onions. Pour mixture over shrimp. Cook in pot over medium heat for 25 minutes. Garnish with peas and pimientos. Serve over rice.

Serves: 4-5
Preparation: 15 minutes
Cooking: 25 minutes

"This popular recipe has been featured on the popular Burdine's Chef's Tour. A companion recipe for chicken and pork is a garlic sauce spiced with oregano. Try this one on other kinds of fish as well."

MOJO CRIOLLO
(CREOLE SAUCE FOR CHICKEN OR PORK)

---

4   cloves garlic
1   t. salt
½   C. oil
    juice from 1 sour orange (or lemon if not
    available)

Crush garlic cloves with salt. Pour oil in frying pan
and heat quickly. Add garlic and juice from orange
(previously heated). Stir thoroughly. When warmed
through, serve over meat with vegetables such as
yuca, ñame, or *malanga.*

Yields: about 1 cup
Preparation: 5 minutes
Cooking: 5 minutes

*"This is not the Southern tomato-based sauce that
you may already be familiar with. It's quite piquante,
and a tablespoon or two added to rice is excellent."*

Malaga
Miami

SANGRÍA

1   bottle Rioja (a Spanish red wine)
8   oz. lemon soda
4   T. sugar
2   whole limes, squeezed
8   oz. mixed fruit cocktail, drained and slightly
      crushed
1   orange, sliced

Pour wine and lemon soda into pitcher. Add sugar, juice from limes, fruit cocktail, and orange slices. Add ice and stir well. Serve in wine goblets.

Serves: 2–4
Preparation: 5 minutes

"A delicious, refreshing Spanish beverage, ideal for any occasion. Goes well with poultry, seafood, and red meat."

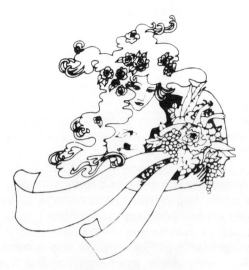

The Spiral

Coral Gables

Inflation may have a spiraling curve, but the prices at The Spiral restaurant have always remained modest. The refreshing, natural foods menu has appealed to everyone from hippies in the 1960s to Rolls Royce owners and, most recently, Christo, the publicity-attracting artist who decorated Miami's Biscayne Bay islands in pink plastic.

This isn't an ordinary "health food" restaurant for Florida. Indeed, owners Hank and Jerry Goldschein would rather not even call it that. The decor is a springy, lively green, with a brightly colored vegetable pattern for wallpaper interspersed with wood paneling and white wrought iron dividers. The surprise as you enter is the slot machine that shows movies for kids of any age.

The restaurant first opened in 1970. When Hank and Jerry became the owners, they kept many of the same items on the menu and added some new ones. Besides the array of seafood tempura dishes, pasta and salads, there's always a "cook's pleasure," usually a hot vegetable special. And if you like vegetable soup, you'll love it at The Spiral—great big chunks of fresh everything, filled up to the top of a bowl of clear but tasty broth. It really is a meal in itself.

"Conscientious cuisine" is what Hank and Jerry call it, serving healthy portions of "basic eats" without pretentiousness. Though meat and chicken don't appear on the menu, seafood does. *Fish Française* is a house specialty prepared as one would prepare veal. The fried buckwheat noodles with vegetables were rated the best health food dish in the area by *South Florida Magazine* (formerly *Miami Magazine*).

The house dressing is made without any dairy products. It's a blend of miso (a soy and rice paste), oil, vinegar, tamari, and a little onion and honey, good enough to be used to flavor just about anything on your plate. Maple syrup or honey are used as sweeteners instead of sugar.

What we enjoyed most of all were the homemade desserts, baked fresh each morning. Banana Carob Pie, Strawberry Pie, Mango-Banana Pie . . . you may rightfully conclude that one bite is worth a thousand reviews.

So put on your jeans or come over in your shorts. The Spiral will be ready to treat your tastebuds.

Directions: The Spiral is at 1630 Ponce de Leon Boulevard. From U.S. 1, turn north on Ponce de Leon Boulevard, going across Miracle Mile until you get to the address. The Spiral is on the west side of the street.

While you're here: The lavish Coral Gables lifestyle became famous during the 1920s, and you can fantasize about the exquisite parties of those times just by driving along the residential streets. Spanish, Mediterranean, and modern architectural styles dominate the estates. The **Players State Theater** *at the nearby* **Coconut Grove Playhouse** *presents star casts in hit shows. The* **Lowe Art Museum Gallery**, *south of the Coral Gables business district on the* **University of Miami** *campus, is one of the prominent art centers of the state, with Renaissance, Baroque, American, and African collections.*

MEATLESS CHILI

1 large onion, chopped
3 green peppers, chopped
1 T. cumin
1 t. salt or to taste
1 t. pepper
1 t. garlic powder
1 T. chili powder or more to taste
1 t. whole thyme
3 tomatoes, chopped
2 cans kidney beans
5 oz. soy burger*
1 small can tomato paste
  cooked rice
  Cheddar cheese, grated

Sauté onions and peppers until tender. Add spices, stir, and add tomatoes. Cook over medium low heat. Add heated beans, soy burger, and tomato paste. Turn off heat. Serve over a large spoonful of rice with grated Cheddar cheese sprinkled on top.

Serves: 4–6
Preparation: 15 minutes
Cooking: 30–45 minutes (the longer time is
          necesary if you use dry kidney beans)

"A delicious variation on an old-time favorite."

*Available in health food stores

MOUSSAKA

3   eggplants

RED SAUCE

1   onion, chopped
     olive oil
2   tomatoes, cut in wedges
1   T. parsley
1   t. oregano
1   t. garlic
1   T. cinnamon
1   T. Tamari*
     salt and pepper to taste
1   small can tomato paste
6   oz. soy burger*

WHITE SAUCE

¼   lb. butter
1   C. white flour
1   pt. milk
1   T. nutmeg
     salt and pepper to taste
2   eggs, beaten
½   lb. ricotta cheese

TO ASSEMBLE:

Peel eggplant, cut into slices, and drop into boiling water, cook for about 10 minutes. For Red Sauce: Saute onions in olive oil, add tomatoes, spices and simmer, about 10 minutes. Add tomato paste and soy burger. Turn off heat and ladle over eggplant. For White Sauce: Mix butter, flour, milk, and seasonings. Stir over medium heat. When mixture thickens, remove from heat. Add eggs and cheese. Ladle over Red Sauce and cook entire dish for 1 hour, uncovered, at 350°F.

Serves: 6–8
Preparation: eggplant—15 minutes;
                         Red Sauce—15 minutes;
                         White Sauce—10 minutes
Cooking: 1 hour

"Another popular natural main course."

˄Available in health food stores or Oriental food stores

BEV'S CABBAGE

cooking oil
1 lb. fettucine noodles, boiled until just tender
1 onion, chopped
5 tomatoes, cut in wedges
1 T. parsley
1 T. garlic powder
1 t. salt
1 t. pepper
1 lb. cottage cheese
½ large head of cabbage, sliced into shreds
butter
1 t. caraway seed
1 t. celery seed
1 t. whole thyme
1 lb. cheese, Swiss and cheddar mixed

Grease baking pan or tray with cooking oil and fill with boiled fettucine noodles. In separate pan sauté onions, tomatoes, parsley, garlic, salt and pepper. Stir cottage cheese into mixture. Spoon over noodles and mix thoroughly. Sauté shredded cabbage in butter with remaining spices, taking care that cabbage doesn't stick to pan. Toss often over medium heat. Spread over noodles. Top with cheese and bake 45 minutes, covered at 350°F.

Serves: 6-8
Preparation: 15-20 minutes
Cooking: 45 minutes

"Do not overcook noodles or cabbage."

MANGO-BANANA PIE

1 baked pie shell
2 or 3 large mangoes, depending upon size
cinnamon and honey to taste
cornstarch
3 T. apple juice
5 bananas, sliced
whipped cream

Prepare the pie shell. Make sure your fruit is very
ripe. The mangoes should be sweet and orange. (The
Spiral currently uses Haitian mangoes.) Slice
mangoes and cook with their own juice in a pot over
medium heat. Add a touch of cinnamon and honey to
taste. Add enough cornstarch to thicken. Add apple
juice and blend well. (Other compatible fruit juice
can be substituted for the apple juice.) The longer
the mangoes are cooked the thicker the mixture will
be. Remove from heat and cool. Mix with sliced
bananas in a separate bowl. Fold into baked pie
shell. Chill and serve topped with whipped cream.

Yields: 1 pie
Preparation: 10 minutes
Cooking: 10-20 minutes plus time to chill and
prepare and bake pie crust

*"This is a heavenly dish. If mangoes are out of
season, try the recipe with canned mangoes and cut
down the cooking time. Combine the mangoes with
peaches or pineapple instead of bananas for another
treat."*

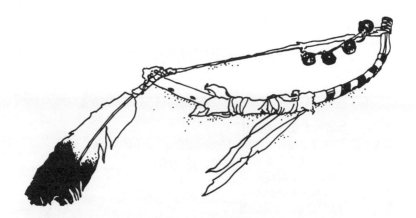

Miccosukee Restaurant

Tamiami Trail (Miami)

Florida's Indian heritage and foodways are characteristic of southeastern United States Indian groups, from whom several tribes in the state are descended. The Miccosukee, for example, come from the Hitichiti-speaking branch of the Creek Nation in the Carolinas and Georgia. They intermingled with native Florida tribes and the Seminoles, who came to the state some years later in the 1700s.

The Miccosukee were recognized in 1962 as a federal Indian tribe, separate from the Seminoles. Both tribes today have complete educational, health and public safety departments, and both benefit from the 104,000-acre State Indian Reservation south of Lake Okeechobee, by the Everglades National Park.

Traditionally, the men in the tribes have been hunters and fishermen. One of the Miccosukee income sources today is derived from the Village and Cultural Center at the reservation, a living example of a real family camp. Visitors along the Tamiami Trail can stop for a taste of Everglades or American dishes at the neighboring Miccosukee Restaurant. Tribal Chairman Buffalo Tiger and his sons Lee (the tribe's public relations expert) and Stephen (an accomplished artist) welcome guests who come to see how the Miccosukee have preserved their old beliefs, religion and customs.

The typical village is composed of several "chickees." These structures consist of an open framework of cypress poles covered with sloping palmetto fronds to keep out the rain. The cooking chickee is the most prominent in the camp, and all of the women prepare meals there over an open fire on the ground. The four cypress poles surrounding the fire by custom are aimed towards the four corners of the earth. You can get an idea of the cooking chickee's importance by understanding that in the matriarchal Indian society, a husband-to-be builds a new chickee in his intended's mother's camp. If his prospective bride accepts him, she places cooking utensils in the chickee and then the ceremony takes place.

The Miccosukee diet traditionally consists of meat, rice and fish, with venison and duck when they are in season. But as land has become less available, some of the old ways of obtaining food have been restricted either by state regulation or as a result of dwindling supplies. Even some of the attitudes toward eating alligator, rattlesnake, and rabbit (once forbidden as food sources) have begun to change over the years. Ask a modern Indian what he likes to eat and the answer is as likely to be a McDonald's hamburger as it is fry bread.

Sofkee, a common Miccosukee and Seminole dish, is traditionally made from cracked hominy, corn kernels treated with wood-ash lye. The soup-like mixture is available throughout the day for people to serve themselves whenever they're hungry. Native fruit trees such as the pigeon plum, seven-year apple, and seagrape are also staples for raw or cooked sweets.

The annual Green Corn Dance held in June is a festival that celebrates the new corn crop, the beginning of the new year for the tribe, and formal induction of the boys into manhood with new names. During the Christmas holiday season the Miccosukees sponsor an Indian Arts Festival among more than 30 tribes from all over the United States. The Village and Restaurant are open to the public year-round.

Directions: *The Miccosukee Restaurant is approximately 40 miles west of Miami on U.S. 41 (Tamiami Trail), on the north side of the road. The Village and Cultural Center are another quarter of a mile west, on the south side of the road.*

While you're here: *Take time to visit the **Village and Cultural Center**, as well as the several Seminole centers along the same road. Both tribes are an important part of Florida's cultural make-up. Gift shop souvenirs include some of the colorful clothing and handiwork made by Indian craftsmen.*

—NOTES—

Miccosukee Restaurant
Tamiami Trail

INDIAN FRY BREAD (MODERN VERSION)

---

2   lbs. self-rising flour
2½ C. water
     cooking oil

In a large bowl, mix water well with flour, using hands. Add additional water if needed. Turn mixture into a dough by kneading it for about 5 minutes. Divide the dough into 3 or 4 pieces. Flatten dough to at least a half-inch thick by turning over and over on palms of hands until each piece is nice and round. Fry in hot oil in skillet, turning when golden. Fry Bread is done when both sides are golden brown. Drain on paper towels. Serve plain or with butter.

Yields: 3–4 servings
Preparation: 10 minutes
Cooking: 5 minutes

"The traditional method calls for fine hominy meal instead of flour, to be mixed with boiling water. We think this way is just fine."

—NOTES—

INDIAN FRIED PUMPKIN BREAD

2   C. self-rising flour (spoon lightly when
      measuring)
1   16-oz. can pumpkin (not pumpkin pie filling)
¾   C. white or brown sugar
      oil for frying

Combine flour, pumpkin, and sugar. Blend well and
refrigerate for 2 hours in order to firm up the dough a
bit. Divide dough into 4 portions. Knead each portion
on a floured board or cloth for a few minutes or until
it can be formed into a cylinder about 8 to 10 inches
long. Cut each cylinder into 6 slices. Flour each slice
and form into a cake no more than a half-inch thick
at the most. Fry the cakes in hot oil. Turn when
bottom side is brown. When both sides are brown,
drain on paper towels and serve *immediately* with
butter and/or maple syrup.

Yields: about 24 slices
Preparation: 10–20 minutes plus time for
                     refrigerating
Cooking: 6–8 minutes

*"This is one of the most popular snacks at the
annual Florida Folk Festival. Instead of deep frying
the cakes, follow the cook's suggestion of using a
well-seasoned cast iron frying pan and filling the pan
a little more than halfway with oil. Try serving these
as a side dish with fried chicken or pork. They are
best when served very hot."*

ORIGINAL INDIAN BURGER

fry bread dough mixture, halved (see recipe,
    page 223)
½   lb. ground beef
½   onion, finely chopped
1   qt. water
    cooking oil for deep frying

Bring to a boil ground beef, onion, and water. Reduce
heat to simmer for 20 minutes. Drain juices from
ground beef. Have the fry bread dough mixture ready,
sized, and rolled flat on aluminum foil dusted with
flour. Take half a handful of the cooked ground beef
mixture and set in middle of fry bread dough. Lift
dough gently around ground beef mixture and
overlap edges of dough, pinching and sealing with
fingers. Deep fry for 6 to 8 minutes. Drain excess oil
on paper towel for a minute. Cut open on top for
condiments, salt and pepper to taste.

Serves: 2
Preparation: 25–30 minutes
Cooking: 6–8 minutes

"Goes great with cole slaw!"

Mangrove Mama's

Sugar Loaf Key

Set at an angle by the side of the road against a clump of trees so that you'd hardly know it was a commercial business, Mangrove Mama's is actually a restaurant in a cottage. It looks more like a vestige of the 1960s than it does a contemporary enterprise.

Though it isn't typical of a "conch" architectural style featuring the wooden "gingerbread" designs so popular in the 19th century, it does have an old-time Keys atmosphere. The floors are concrete, the bar is made from seasoned Dade pine, there's a porch dining area and a brick fireplace, and tables are decked with cotton tablecloths with faded fruit patterns. You've heard that the atmosphere in the Keys is casual and laid back? Here's proof. Mangrove Mama's "feels" like a beach bar, but creative, homestyle cooking is the emphasis, not the bar.

Join several natives at the counter—there are no strangers here—and prepare for a treat, from conch fritters with more conch per bite than you may have sampled elsewhere, to the taste sensation of freshly broiled fish with "Dixie" fries, to the unexpected pleasure of nutmeg shavings that enliven the desserts. Conch steak is fixed with white wine and lemon juice for an exceptional variation on a popular local dish. Garlic is served on the side with everything, "a way of life" at Mangrove Mama's. Sometimes home-baked goods are served from Mama LaBomba's, nearby. The menu varies according to "season," summer lasting for seven months and winter temperatures being not much different.

Those open-door breezes whisking past your ear while you eat may be something more than a gentle wind. You see, Mangrove Mama was originally the name of a boat owned by the restaurant's first owner, Captain Edward Waldon Linton (1880–1956). Rumor has it that his spirit still haunts the site and the building itself, which has withstood many a hurricane over the past 30 or so years.

Visitors who are not native conchs can only relax and enjoy the food and the company, sit around and hear tales about how Key Westerners came to be known as conchs, and let their imagination run free over the different colors of the waters of the Atlantic Ocean and the Gulf of Mexico.

With a little help from Mangrove Mama's natural food, it won't take long for your Keys fantasies to become reality.

Directions: *Mangrove Mama's is at Mile Marker 20. Take U.S. 1 to this marker, on the west side of the road, just a short drive north of Key West.*

While you're here: *The Keys are a nature lover's paradise.*
Here along the lower part of the chain are the state park at
Bahia Honda, Big Pine Key *with its tiny deer and tall*
Caribbean pines, snorkeling and skin-diving along **Looe Key**
Reef *(a national marine sanctuary accessible only by water,*
southwest of Big Pine), camping facilities, and woods.
Sugar Loaf Key *was named after Indian middens (refuse*
heaps) that looked like sugar loaves to the early settlers.
Nature tours and seaplane trips originate from the Sugar
Loaf Lodge.

On the last key to the west
Underneath an eagle's nest,
Dig a fathom in the rotted tier.
The chests have rotted from their bales
But the yellow gold will prove the tales
About the MANGROVE BUCCANEER.

© 1975 Anhinga Roost Music (SESAC)
(Dale Crider)
Printed by permission

Mangrove Mama
Sugar Loaf Key

CONCH STEAK

---

1   conch* steak, fresh or frozen
     flour
1   egg, beaten
     clarified butter**
½   t. lemon juice
1   T. dry white wine
     salt to taste

Butterfly conch steak by cutting out the vein, sliding
knife down each side, and opening steak out to each
side. Tenderize by pounding with mallet or back of a
knife. Dredge steak in flour, dip in beaten egg, and
back again into flour. Sauté over medium heat in
clarified butter, about 45 seconds on each side. Add
lemon juice, wine, and salt to taste. Serve
immediately.

Serves: 1
Preparation: 15–30 minutes (includes 10–15 minutes
                for tenderizing conch)
Cooking: 2 minutes

*"The butter-lemon juice-wine combination is a
perfect flavor enhancer for the conch. Try this sauce
with other seafood as well. If conch is frozen, defrost
it quickly under cold running water. Try serving this
dish with steamed new potatoes or home fries."*

*Available at most seafood markets, or write publisher for name of
supplier in your area

**See Glossary

CONCH FRITTERS

½	lb. conch, tenderized
1	large onion
1	sweet red pepper
⅓	t. salt
⅓	t. black pepper
¼	t. garlic powder or to taste
1	t. baking powder
⅓-½	C. white flour
1	egg, slightly mixed
	oil to deep fat fry

Coarsely grind conch in food processor or meat grinder and place in separate mixing bowl. Repeat for onions and pepper. In a separate bowl add salt, pepper, garlic powder, and baking powder to flour and stir to mix. Add conch, onions, and pepper to dry mixture. Add egg and mix well. You may have to add more flour to bind the ingredients. Form mixture into 16 fritters. Heat oil to 350°F. and fry fritters, a few at a time, until golden. Drain and serve with cocktail sauce, *fresh* horseradish, or lemon juice.

Yields: 16
Preparation: 20 minutes
Cooking: 10-15 minutes

"You can use this recipe to make clam fritters as well, but you will have to use a little more flour for binding. The trick to these fritters is to use just enough flour to bind the conch and the other ingredients together. What a great way to savor real conch flavor!"

DIXIE FRIES

4   potatoes, cut in ⅜-inch strips, square on ends
water
vegetable oil (such as soybean)

Soak potato strips in 100°F. water for 15 minutes to take out excess starch and prevent turning black. Drain water. Pat dry. Fry a few at a time in 300°F. oil for 45 seconds. Cool at room temperature. Store and re-fry at 375°F. to desired brownness for another minute or less. Fries should be crispy outside, tender and sweet inside, and a rich, golden-orange color.

Serves: 4
Preparation: 20 minutes
Cooking: 2 minutes per batch

"These fries can be made with or without the skins."

ONION RINGS WITH SESAME SEEDS

2   large onions
      salt
2   C. flour
1   T. sesame seeds, or more to taste
1   egg, whipped slightly
1   C. ice water
3-4   ice cubes
¼   t. white pepper

Slice onions into ½-inch rings. Separate rings and lightly salt. Let stand for 10 minutes at room temperature until onion rings are damp and slightly limp. Mix sesame seeds with 1 cup of flour and set aside. Make batter by mixing the egg with the second cup of flour, ice water, ice cubes and pepper. Dip onion rings in flour, then in batter. Fry in deep oil heated to 375°F. for about 1 minute, just until crispy brown outside.

Serves: 2-4
Preparation: 15 minutes
Cooking: 1 minute per batch

"Try this technique and your batter will adhere beautifully to the onion rings. If you have extra batter, dip other fresh vegetables into it and prepare in the same way. Broccoli, mushrooms, or cauliflower come out 'tempura style.' "

MICHAEL'S BANANAS

2   oz. clarified butter*
2   pinches *fresh* ground nutmeg
2   ripe bananas, sliced
⅓   fresh whole pineapple, cored and cut in chunks,
      or 1 small can chunk pineapple
2   T. fresh lemon juice
4   scoops vanilla ice cream
      ground nutmeg for garnish

Heat butter in a skillet. Add nutmeg and bananas and sauté for 1 minute over medium heat. When bananas begin to "melt," add pineapple and lemon juice. Stir and sauté another minute. Serve in individual dishes with a scoop of vanilla ice cream over each. Sprinkle nutmeg lightly over the ice cream and serve.

Serves: 4
Preparation: 20 minutes (includes time for coring
               and preparing fresh pineapple)
Cooking: 3 minutes

"This dish is a refreshing and cooling dessert, especially in hot weather. The aromatic spice of the fresh ground nutmeg makes it superlative!"

*See Glossary

233

Half Shell Raw Bar, Key West, Florida

Half Shell Raw Bar

Key West

All of Key West is good for immersing yourself in local color, but one of your most memorable experiences may very well be at the Half Shell Raw Bar. Here's where many commercial fishermen congregate, and lunch is as likely to be something unexpected, fresh from the catch, as it is to be something already on the menu.

Fishing is pretty much a way of life, a *raison d'être*. Strike up a conversation with a chap anywhere in town, and chances are good he's either done some pretty serious fishing or is thinking about it. And chances are even better he'll be a regular at the Half Shell, along with folks from all walks of life and just about every population segment you can name in the Keys. It's truly a place where anyone can go with anyone and be comfortable.

The Half Shell Raw Bar is something like a beach bar, with brick and concrete floors, picnic tables with old hatch covers for tops, and nautical decor lining the walls and ceilings—sponges, lanterns, fish heads, and lines. It's a tradition that whenever the sightseeing train whistles out front, whoever is sitting nearest the line attached to a ship's bell at

235

the counter must reach up to the line to ring the bell. It's also a tradition to take snapshots of the people in your party posing at the "photo board" in front of the restaurant.

Owners Karl Coxhead and Paul Tripp, originally from Montreal and Michigan, respectively, manage to keep all the commotion in tow. Paul had previously operated a local guest house, and Karl, who had vacationed many times in Key West, grew up in a family that had always been in the restaurant business. Paul's dad works with them here, too. Karl, by the way, is also a mime, and you'll see him in local theatrical performances when he has the time.

You won't find any run-of-the-mill seafood preparations here, so you mustn't be reluctant to try new taste sensations. For example: grilled swordfish, outstanding conch chowder, "pink gold" (shrimp), snapper almondine, mako or black tip shark, shark bites, smoked conch, oysters from Apalachicola, barbecue tuna salad. . .whatever the seas may yield. Those fried things that look like onion rings and are seasoned with garlic and lime? They're squid rings, unexpectedly tasty.

One thing you *won't* find on the Half Shell's menu is turtle, as the species of sea turtle found in local waters is protected by Florida law. There's a great ecological sensitivity about marine life in the Keys, and you'll be encouraged to adopt those concerns as your own when you realize that human systems are delicately interwoven with all other living systems.

In the final analysis, if it's good, fresh, and permissible by law, the Half Shell will have your choice of seafood.

Directions: The Half Shell Raw Bar is at No. 1 Land's End Village. Take U.S. 1 all the way into town to Duval Street and turn right. Turn right again on Caroline, then left on Margaret Street all the way to the end.

While you're here: Just across from the restaurant are the historic Turtle Kraals and museum. "Kraals" is a Dutch word meaning holding pen or corral. Stakes used to be driven into the ocean and the turtles destined to be made into soup were dropped into the pens to be held for slaughter. Today, the Department of Natural Resources periodically sends 50 young sea turtles to the marina in an effort to prevent the species' extinction.

SQUID RINGS

**(Allow 2 to 3 hours to marinate and 1 hour for
    breading to set)**
2   **lbs. squid***

MARINADE

    juice of 3 Key limes (may substitute other limes)
3   **cloves of garlic, crushed and chopped fine**
½   **t. freshly ground black pepper**

Clean squid* and cut into ½-inch rings. Mix with
marinade ingredients and marinate 2 to 3 hours.

BATTER

2   **eggs**
1   **C. milk**
1   **C. flour**
1   **lb. fine cracker meal**

Prepare an egg wash (eggs and milk mixed). Dust
squid with flour, dip first in egg wash, then in
cracker meal. Refrigerate 1 hour for breading to set.
Deep fry to a golden brown.

Serves: 4-6
Preparation: Marinate 2-3 hours, refrigerate
                 breading 1 hour
Cooking: 5-10 minutes

**"The flavor is unusual—a popular dish at the Half
Shell!"**

*To clean squid, remove the spiny translucent portion and then pull head
and legs from the envelope-like covering. Peel skin from the body and cut
across the head above the eyes.

CONCH FRITTERS

1 lb. conch meat*, fresh or frozen, tenderized
½ large green pepper
½ medium onion
1 pickled jalapeño pepper, finely chopped (or any other hot pepper)
½ 1-lb. box or less of Aunt Jemima's Complete Pancake Mix
peanut oil for frying (or vegetable oil)

Coarsely grind *tenderized* conch meat into mixing bowl, either with a meat grinder or a food processor. Be careful to keep the juice. Dice green pepper and onion into ¹⁄₁₆-inch squares. Place green pepper and onion in a sieve and blanch 1 minute in boiling water. Add green pepper, onion, jalapeño, and pancake mix to conch. Mix thoroughly, adding water if necessary. Allow to set for 30 minutes. With small scoop or hands, make balls about 1 inch in diameter. Heat oil to 350°F. Deep fry fritters, a few at a time, until deep golden in color. Serve with cocktail sauce or chili sauce.

Serves: 8–10
Preparation: 10 minutes (plus 30 minutes for batter to rest)
Cooking: approximately 3 minutes per batch

"If you can't get fresh conch, don't be afraid to use frozen. Defrost it quickly by running it under cold water. Be sure to pound the meat with a mallet to tenderize, as grinding doesn't do the job. These fritters make delectable hors d'oeuvres as well as a special treat for the family."

*Available at most seafood markets, or write us for the name of a supplier in your area.

Half Shell Raw Bar
Key West

SMOKED FISH DIP

1   lb. smoked fish* (kingfish, marlin, tuna or sailfish)
1   stalk of celery
¼   onion
    Tabasco sauce
    mayonnaise
    lime juice

Grind smoked fish, celery and onion into a mixing bowl, using the paddle of the mixer. Blend at a slow speed. Add enough mayonnaise to bind. Season with Tabasco and lime juice.

Serves: 6–10 as an hors d'oeuvre
Preparation: 5 minutes

"Serve with crackers or in lettuce cups."

*Be sure to remove bones.

KEY LIME PIE

CRUST

4	oz. softened butter
2	C. graham cracker crumbs
¼	t. vanilla extract

FILLING

4	eggs, separated
1	6-oz. can sweetened condensed milk
¼	C. Key lime juice

MERINGUE

	reserved egg whites
1	t. vanilla extract
1	t. cream of tartar
¼	t. salt
¾	C. super-fine sugar

For crust: Blend softened butter with graham cracker crumbs and vanilla extract. Spread and press mixture around bottom and sides of a 9-inch pie pan.

For filling: Blend egg yolks and milk, then add Key lime juice. Fold into pie shell.

For meringue: Beat egg whites until frothy. Add
vanilla extract, cream of tartar and salt and beat
slightly. Add sugar gradually, beating well after each
addition. Continue beating until mixture forms stiff
peaks. Swirl over pie filling and bake at 400°F. until
meringue is brown, about 7 to 10 minutes.
Refrigerate immediately.

Yields: 1 9-inch pie
Preparation: 15–20 minutes
Cooking: 7–10 minutes

*"Key Lime Pie is a real Florida treat. Fresh Key limes
are found in season in some Florida supermarkets.
Buy them when they are available, squeeze and
freeze the juice for future use."*

Pepe's Café

Key West

For those who think of Key West as a kind of romantic retreat, a haven to quietly go about doing your own thing and without anyone bothering you, there's a place for you.

For those who would rather get a feel for the island's leisure pace over friendly chit-chat, a newspaper and coffee, amid some of the native plants and flowers, there's a place for you.

And for those who prefer to take their time over a light, nicely prepared meal in a slightly offbeat, funky environment, there's a place for you.

All of these needs can be met at Pepe's Café, the oldest eating place in Key West, in business since 1909. It has appealed all these years to local political gurus, kids, couples, artistic types, and whoever else wanders in. It's been at its present location since 1962 and is now owned by Molly and Eddie Hogan, who came here from Martha's Vineyard in 1975. Molly is an artist herself, and you'll see some of her pen and ink sketches by the entrance to the café.

You'll also notice the giant ceiling fan, nearly 10 feet in diameter. It's constructed from a washing machine motor and handmade paddles. "Son of" the giant ceiling fan, several feet away, is just an ordinary unit.

The ambiance created by the rustic wood paneling on the interior, wooden booths and fireplace invites you to make yourself at home. Outside, protected from roadside passers-by via canvas and a fence, is the café's greatest charm, a patio garden shaded by rubber trees and multi-colored bougainvillea. In the back is the café's own herb garden, which supplies the freshest seasonings.

Menu fare changes with the season, lighter dishes being served in the summer, but some are served all year. A reviewer from the *Philadelphia Enquirer* raved about the chicken livers and scrambled eggs; *Cosmopolitan* liked the chili. The variations on a theme performed with pancakes and omelets are quite satisfying, and you'll be torn between choosing the Cuban coffee pie or the Cuban banana cream pie. Dinners and main courses show a lot of imagination, with occasional appearances by "guest chefs." Key limes for pie are home-grown, and the bananas come from a local source.

Do partake!

Directions: *Pepe's Café is at 806 Caroline Street. Take U.S. 1 all the way into town. Turn right on Duval Street, the main downtown avenue. Then turn right on Caroline Street, to address. Pepe's Café is on the right.*

While you're here: *There are so many things to see and do in the historic Old Town. Sightseeing trains are a good way to begin. Then you can go back to favorite spots on your own, comfortably walking or bicycling around the entire island.* **Ernest Hemingway, Tennessee Ernie Williams,** *and* **John James Audubon** *all spent time here, and their homes are restored and open to the public. The preponderance of 19th-century conch-style wooden architecture, which blends intricate Victorian design with practical construction with an eye to the weather, makes you wonder why anyone would ever want to build any other way here. In 1870 Key West was Florida's largest city, but today, the "Conch Republic" is known primarily as a resort area, perhaps the most romantic in the state. Here's the perfect wedding just as our publisher did it: get married on a yacht on one of the romantic channels, have it all catered by the locals, then sail off for a 10 hour cruise!*

AVOCADO-BACON-SWISS CHEESE OMELET

3 eggs
3 T. half-and half
   dash Tabasco
   salt and pepper to taste
2 T. ripe avocado, diced
1 oz. grated Swiss cheese
1 slice crisp bacon

Combine first 4 ingredients and beat well. Pour into well-oiled omelet pan and cook over medium heat until puffy. Add avocado, cheese, and crumbled bacon. Serve either open-faced or folded over.

Serves: 1
Preparation: 2 minutes
Cooking: 3 minutes

"Let the cheese melt a bit before serving."

HOUSE DRESSING

¼	head garlic, peeled
⅛	C. water
½-1	bunch dill, chopped (stems removed)
1½	cucumbers, peeled and cut up
1½	C. sour cream
1½	C. mayonnaise

Blend garlic with water in a blender or food processor. Add dill and cucumbers, then the sour cream. Blend thoroughly. Pour into a bowl and stir in mayonnaise. Add salt and pepper to taste. Store in refrigerator.

Yields: about ½ gallon
Preparation: 10 minutes

"This would also taste good over leftover or cold poached fish!"

HUEVOS RANCHEROS SAUCE

¼ C. onions, chopped
¼ C. green pepper, chopped
1 T. vegetable oil
   salt and pepper
   pinch of basil and garlic powder
1 t. cumin
1 28-oz. can crushed tomatoes

Sauté onions and peppers in oil until soft. Add spices and tomatoes. Continue cooking over low heat until flavors meld.

Yields: about 3 cups
Preparation: 5 minutes
Cooking: 10 minutes

"This sauce can be served over eggs or grits. We baked thin pork chops for 35 minutes with 1 tablespoon of sauce per chop to keep them moist and then poured the rest of the sauce over the chops before serving. Add a few drops of Tabasco for extra dash."

Pepe's Café
Key West

SEAFOOD STIR FRY

---

4   T. peanut oil
2   C. any combination shrimp, lobster, or crab
      (cleaned)
1   C. sliced mushrooms
¾   C. sliced green pepper
2   C. bok choy or Chinese cabbage
2   C. mungbean sprouts
1   C. shredded cabbage (red or green)
½   C. sliced celery
½   C. sliced carrots
½   C. sliced broccoli or yellow squash
½   C. sherry
¼   C. Tamari*
½   t. ground ginger

Heat 2 tablespoons peanut oil in wok over high heat. Stir fry seafood and remove to hot platter. Drain pan. Heat remaining 2 tablespoons of oil. Add vegetables, sherry, Tamari, and ginger. Stir fry until vegetables are done, about 3–5 minutes. Add hot seafood to vegetables and serve over rice.

Serves: 6–8
Preparation: 20–30 minutes
Cooking: 10 minutes

"Use any amount of vegetables that appeal to you."

*Tamari can be purchased in health food stores. Soy sauce can be used as a substitute.

247

Cutting down the Sabal Palm "Swamp Cabbage," Florida (Florida
State Archives)

Flora and Ella's Restaurant

LaBelle

Remember in old-time movies and stories about Americana how there was always one place in town where you could go for just about all your business—to buy groceries, mail a letter, buy a bus ticket, purchase a few sundries, sip an ice cream soda or malt for two, or stop in for dinner? Those places are just about gone now, except for an occasional "find." Flora and Ella's Restaurant is such a treasure.

That's Flora Hampton and Ella Burchard, and various relatives who make up the Poole family which is now in its seventh generation in this part of Florida. About the only people who were in LaBelle before Flora and Ella's grandparents were the Caloosa Indians, who were driven out during the Seminole Wars. Settlement in LaBelle peaked in 1880 as steamboats along the Caloosahatchee River brought new residents. The restaurant traces its beginnings to the grocery store and meat market run by Flora and Ella's parents during the Depression.

The big events of each decade all affected business, from the devastating hurricanes of the 1920s to the Great Depression and World War II. The restaurant actually opened in a log cabin in 1933. Its immediate predecessor was a little hamburger stand with hand-carved pine furnishings.

Today the restaurant represents a trip back in time, with almost everything the same as it's always been. Even the Western Union office the Burchard family runs is the oldest in Florida. And the menu includes pioneer delights, with more ways to enjoy swamp cabbage than anyone has a right to imagine.

Other Cracker food specialties at Flora and Ella's do justice to Southern and soul food traditions, all fixed the same way as they've been since the 1940s. No doubt their knowledge of seasonings has been influenced by their grandmother, who, back in the 1880s, was a doctor of sorts and familiar with all the herbs that grew in the woods nearby. But it's their luscious pies that they're *most* known for, says Ella.

Whether or not you have Florida roots yourself, this is one place where you can enrich your understanding of the state's history and small town heritage.

Directions: Flora and Ella's Restaurant is on SR 29, at the junction of Bridge and Fort Thompson. LaBelle is about 25 miles east of Fort Myers, reached from I-75 by going east on SR 80. From 80, turn north on 29. The restaurant is on the west side of the road, a block and a half before you get to the bridge.

While you're here: The area is renowned for its annual **Swamp Cabbage Festival** *in February. About 45 miles to the east in Lake Harbor is the* **Miami Canal Lock** *state historic site and museum, with displays that interpret Everglades reclamation and conservation programs. Flooding from Lake Okeechobee and hurricanes have been consistent problems and have been immortalized in a song by Florida's "Black Hat Troubadour" Will McLean: "Lord, hold back the waters of Lake Okeechobee/Lake Okeechobee's water is cold/When wild winds are blowin' across Okeechobee/They're seeking and looking for other poor souls." Today, acres of reclaimed lands are harvested frequently during the year for vegetables and sugar.*

Flora and Ella'a
LaBelle

SWAMP CABBAGE

2 or 3 meaty pieces of ham hock or other seasoning
      meat
2 to 4 swamp cabbages* (or 2 cans hearts of palm,
      rinsed and drained)
      water
      salt to taste
      garlic salt to taste
      black pepper to taste
      rice (optional)
      dash of Tabasco sauce

Cover the ham hock with water and simmer for
30 minutes in order to create a stock. Place swamp
cabbage in pot and add additional water to cover, if
needed. Taste to see if salt is needed. Add garlic salt
and pepper. Cover and bring to a slow boil. Reduce
heat and simmer for 30 minutes or until cabbage is
tender. If amount of cabbage is limited or if you prefer
it without much "juice," add a cup or two of rice after
cabbage boils. Stir occasionally to prevent sticking.
Add water, if necessary, to maintain desired texture.
About 2 minutes before serving, add a dash of
Tabasco. Stir well.

Serves: 3–6
Preparation: 30 minutes
Cooking: 3–45 minutes

*"If you are using canned hearts of palm: simmer with
stock, garlic salt, and pepper until just heated
through. Add Tabasco and rice (which has been
cooked separately) just before serving."*

*Raw swamp cabbage must be cooked down like greens. Allow 1 gallon
greens per 2 quarts desired. See Appendix for information on obtaining
this state-protected plant.

251

Flora and Ella's
LaBelle

SWAMP CABBAGE SALAD

(Allow 6 oz. after preparation per serving)

raw swamp cabbage* or canned (drained and
    rinsed)
salt water (strong)
hard-boiled egg
pickles
mayonnaise
other fresh salad vegetables

If using raw cabbage, first soak in salt water about
20 minutes. Drain and rinse. Add remaining
ingredients and mix.

Preparation: 25 minutes

*"If you prefer, substitute oil and vinegar for
mayonnaise. You'll like the crunchiness."*

*One head will serve 8 with hearty appetites. See Appendix for information
on obtaining this state-protected plant.

*Flora and Ella's
LaBelle*

SWAMP CABBAGE WITH POTATOES

raw swamp cabbage* (allow 6 oz. after preparation
   per serving)
salt water (strong)
potatoes, peeled and quartered
cured ham, cut in 2-inch pieces
salt and pepper to taste
onions (optional)

Soak raw cabbage in strong salt water 20 minutes.
Drain and rinse well. Add remaining ingredients.
Cook over medium heat until done.

Serves: depends on size of cabbage head
Preparation: 25 minutes
Cooking: 30 minutes

*"If you use canned hearts of palm, just drain and
rinse before using. (Do not soak.)"*

*See Appendix for information on obtaining this state-protected plant. Or
substitute canned hearts of palm.

253

Flora and Ella's
LaBelle

SOUR CREAM CAKE

---

1 C. butter (do not substitute)
3 C. sugar
6 eggs, separated, whites stiffly beaten
3 C. all-purpose flour
1 C. sour cream
¼ t. baking soda
1 t. vanilla
1 t. almond extract

Cream butter and sugar until very creamy. Add egg yolks, 1 at a time, beating well after each addition. Sift flour 3 times. Add baking soda to sour cream and stir. Add flour and sour cream alternately to butter-sugar-egg mixture. Blend well after each addition. Add flavorings and fold in stiffly beaten egg whites. Pour into well-greased, lightly floured tube pan. Bake 1½ hours at 300°F. Cool on a rack.

Yields: 1 cake
Preparation: about 15–20 minutes
Cooking: 1½ hours

"A combination of sugar, cinnamon, and nuts can be sprinkled on top of cake about 20 minutes before cake is done."

LEMON MERINGUE PIE

2	C. sugar
1	C. water
¼	C. lemon juice
1	t. lemon extract
¼	C. butter or margarine
	pinch salt
1	C. water
5	egg yolks (save whites for meringue)
8	T. cornstarch
1	baked 9¼-inch pie shell

Combine first 6 ingredients in a medium-size saucepan. Bring to a boil over medium to medium high heat, stirring occasionally. Meanwhile, mix second cup of water with cornstarch and egg yolks. Blend with fork until smooth. Pour quickly into boiling mixture, stirring constantly until thickened. Pour into pie shell, cool slightly, and top with meringue (see recipe page 257).

Yields: 1 9¼-inch pie
Preparation: 15 minutes
Cooking: 10 minutes

"Out of this world in richness! It makes a beautiful presentation to set before your family and friends."

COCONUT PIE

---

1   9-inch baked pie shell
1   C. shredded coconut
1¼ C. sugar
1   13-oz. can evaporated milk
1   13-oz. can water (reserve half)
1   t. vanilla
1   T. butter or margarine
    pinch salt
5   T. cornstarch
5   egg yolks (save whites for meringue)
1   recipe for meringue (see page 257)

Prepare pie shell, bake, and cool.
Combine next 7 ingredients in a medium-size
saucepan. Bring to a boil over medium to medium
high heat, stirring occasionally. Meanwhile, mix
remaining half can of water with cornstarch and egg
yolks. Blend with a fork until smooth. Pour
cornstarch-egg yolk mixture quickly into boiling
mixture. Stir constantly until thickened. Pour into pie
shell. Pile meringue onto hot pie filling and bake for
8 minutes at 400°F.

Yields: 1 9-inch pie
Preparation: 10 minutes
Cooking: about 10 minutes

*"Forget your diet! This is too good to pass up. It's a
feast for the eyes as well and will assure you a
reputation as a pie baker extraordinaire!"*

MERINGUE FOR COCONUT OR LEMON PIE

5   egg whites
½   t. vanilla for coconut pie or ¼ t. lemon extract for
    lemon pie
¼   t. cornstarch
¼   t. cream of tartar
    pinch salt
½   C. sugar

Combine all ingredients except sugar in a large
mixing bowl and beat until frothy. Add sugar
gradually and continue beating until stiff peaks form
and sugar is totally dissolved. Spoon meringue over
pie, making sure edges are sealed with meringue.
Bake for about 8 minutes in a 400°F. oven, just until
lightly browned. Watch baking time carefully. Cool
pie gradually in a warm place away from drafts.

Yields: meringue for 1 pie
Preparation: about 10 minutes
Cooking: about 8 minutes

*"Start the meringue while pie mixture is cooking. The
pie filling should be hot when you cover it with the
meringue."*

ELLA'S PECAN PIE

1   9-inch pie shell, unbaked
5   eggs
1   C. white sugar
1   C. white corn syrup
¼   t. salt
1   t. vanilla
2   T. melted butter or margarine
1   C. chopped pecans (or 1 C. chopped walnuts)

Prepare a 9-inch pie shell. Do not bake.
Break eggs into a large mixing bowl and beat well.
Add sugar, corn syrup, salt, vanilla, and butter, one
ingredient at a time, beating well after each addition.
Stir in pecans. Pour into pie shell and bake about
1 hour at 350ºF. Pie filling will set and be firm when
done.

Yields: 1 9-inch pie
Preparation: about 10 minutes (plus time for making
                pie shell)
Cooking: about 1 hour

*"This is one of the best pecan pies we've ever
tasted. The extra eggs make it very light and
heavenly. Serve warm or at room temperature. Add
whipped cream or ice cream if you insist on gilding
the lily!"*

Gator Grill

Marco Island

So much development has occurred on Marco Island in recent years that it's hard to find an "older" neighborhood or business area. Condominiums with spectacular views of the Gulf of Mexico crowd the land along the waterfront, and suburban-style resort clubs have sprung up all over the island.

But if you follow the directions below very carefully, you'll find a discovery in a pleasant though otherwise undistinguished office building. The Gator Grill's parking lot faces a marshy pond where you can listen to the bullfrogs gulping in harmony all day and all night, and yes, there *are* alligators in the pond, so don't take your pet for a walk there.

The 'gator served at the Grill has on occasion been caught right in the Grill's own back yard, but be thou hereby advised that state laws are *very* strict regarding who may catch alligators, under what circumstances, and how they may be sold. The Grill even posts its own sign that reads "Genuine Florida 'gator meat sold by special permission of state," specifically by the Game and Fresh Water Fish Commission (see page 286).

Larry Amrhein, owner of the Grill, says most of his 'gators come from Naples. He cuts the tail into fillets when the licensed trappers bring in the meat, then re-bags and freezes it until it's to be cooked. Butchers in Naples do the grinding and mixing with other ingredients to make 'gator burgers.

The rest of the menu is seasonal and standard grill and sandwich fare, but at great low prices. Larry doesn't want to see business go elsewhere, so he's careful to keep the prices down. Depending on the ups and downs of the economy, there can be lines of construction workers willing to eat lunch standing up when there's no room to sit down.

While you're filling up on the eats, take a look at the garage sale items neatly on display in one corner of the restaurant. At one time or another, there's been everything from a pot-bellied stove to a teddy bear to a golf cart and who knows what other odds 'n' ends. If you happen to be a "snowbird," you'll grin at another sign claiming a "$5 minimum charge to listen to 'how beautiful, cheap and big everything is up north.' "

Except the 'gators . . . .

Directions: The Gator Grill is at 30 Marco Lake Drive. To get to Marco Island, take SR 92 from Royal Palm Hammock at U.S. 41 (Tamiami Trail), or CR 951 from Belle Meade at 41. Once you're on the island, take 951 to the intersection with Bald Eagle Road (CR 953) and turn left. When you see the United Telephone Company building and antenna, turn left onto Marco Lake Drive and follow the small yellow signs that direct you to the Gator Grill at the back office buildings by the lake. If you're coming from SR 92, turn right on CR 953 (Bald Eagle) and right at the phone company.

While you're here: Marco Island is great for shelling and even greater for watching the sunsets. Though it's a little bit of a drive to get from Marco, at the northern tip of the Ten Thousand Islands, to Everglades City, it's worth the time. You can take an Everglades boat tour or fishing trip or visit the **Everglades National Park**, which contains almost a million and a half acres of land and water with all manner of mangrove trees, tropical flora and rare birds, game fish and reptiles.

'GATOR BURGER

2-2½   lbs. 'gator meat*
¼   lb. lean, mild Italian sausage in bulk form
1-2   eggs
½   C. bread crumbs
        salt, pepper, garlic, onion salt, Accent to taste

Grind 'gator meat, normally a tough, fine and fat-free meat. Add sausage to hold meat together. Work in eggs, bread crumbs, and seasonings to taste. Mix thoroughly. Make patties and grill, preferably on a flat surface indoors. Turn carefully with a spatula to avoid crumbling. Serve on a roll and sink your teeth into the 'gator!

Serves: 4 to 6
Preparation: 15 minutes
Cooking: 15 to 20 minutes

"Not your everyday kind of ordinary burger—delicious!"

*Only state-licensed trappers may catch alligators in Florida, and only restaurants may serve or sell the meat, pre-cooked. This recipe is presented so you may better enjoy it at the Gator Grill.

State Farmers Market Restaurant

Fort Myers

Farmers' markets are among the best ways to experience a state's local color and farm flavor. Families and truckers display their produce in stalls and pretty near hawk their pickin's like there's no tomorrow. The only way to get anything fresher is to be there on the farm and pick it yourself.

At the State Farmers Market in Fort Myers, several intermediate steps between farm and retail establishment take place, namely, weighing, inspection and shipping. The adjacent restaurant has catered to truckers, people in the food industry, families, and local business employees for more than a quarter of a century. Though the restaurant is medium sized, it seems more like a place for a large family gathering, with guests calling out across the room to each other as they see familiar faces.

When Bill Barnwell became the owner a few years ago, he kept the same recipes, staff, and customs the restaurant always had. It's a tradition to start every meal with an oversized basket of fresh cornbread and muffins, some 2,000 of which are consumed on a typical weekend day. And no one will bat an eyelash if you pop a couple into a napkin to take with you, either.

As you might expect, the vegetables are country-fresh dishes such as turnip greens and squash casserole when they're in season. For a return to the spirit of the good ol' days of Sunday dinner after church, you'll feast on all the old Southern favorites, accompanied by three vegetables. It's worth the wait. Even if you find yourself sharing table space with another family, it's a fine way to make new friends.

Popular local seafood favorites start with Okeechobee catfish and the ubiquitous mullet and grouper.

For a "slice of life," Florida-style, try the State Farmers Market Restaurant.

Directions: The State Farmers Market Restaurant is at 2736 Edison Avenue. From I-75, take the Anderson Avenue exit west. Turn south on Fowler Street (Alternate U.S. 41), then west on Edison Avenue to address. The restaurant is on the south side of the road. Or you can take U.S. 41 (Cleveland Avenue) and turn east on Anderson.

While you're here: Some of the main drives in Fort Myers are lined with block after block of stately royal palm trees and are some of the most scenic streets you'll see in any Florida city. Ride around, then visit the **Thomas Edison Winter Home,** complete with laboratory, botanical gardens and museum. The giant banyan tree on its 14-acre estate is the largest in the state. On 41 south of Fort Myers is an unusual **Honeybee Factory** and glass-enclosed observatory where you can watch the bees "in production" without getting stung.

OKRA AND TOMATOES

½   stick margarine or butter
1   lb. tomatoes, quartered
2   lbs. okra, trimmed and sliced if large
1   onion, chopped
1   T. sugar
    salt and pepper to taste

Melt margarine or butter in a pot. Add tomatoes, okra, and onion. Bring to a boil. Cover and let simmer until okra is tender. While the vegetables are cooking, mash the tomatoes from time to time. Season with sugar and salt and pepper to taste.

Serves: 4–6
Preparation: 5 minutes
Cooking: 30–45 minutes

"If you can't find fresh okra, use frozen, but rinse before cooking to remove the ice crystals."

FRESH COLLARD GREENS

---

    collard greens
    enough water to cover
2   small ham hocks or 1 fat back, chopped
¼   C. bacon drippings
¼   C. sugar
    salt and pepper to taste

Wash greens at least four times to remove sand. Cut greens in small pieces. Place in pot and cover with water. Add ham hocks or fat back. Gently boil for 2½ hours or until greens are tender. Add bacon drippings, sugar, salt, and pepper to taste.

Serves: 6
Preparation: 10 minutes
Cooking: 2½ hours

"Drain greens before adding the seasonings. This is an authentic Southern dish!"

Buttonwood Bar-B-Q

Sanibel

For Greg and Diane Steger, making the career switch from unrelated occupations into the restaurant business must have been in their stars. When they moved to Florida from Detroit, they were looking for a rewarding business to get into. Trained as a respiratory therapist, Diane had previously sold tropical fish, but that was their sole prior connection—and a remote one, at that—to anything resembling seafood. Her mother and father owned the Santiva Cottages, across from the convenience store next door to where the restaurant now stands. After she and Greg got settled in their new home, she began smoking mullet at the Santiva Mini-Mart nearby.

Obviously, she was doing something right. After all, she admits, she *does* love to cook. Business picked up, and soon the whole family was involved. They expanded the menu. Then, when Greg and Diane realized that barbecue was something missing on Sanibel and Captiva Islands, they decided to open their Buttonwood Bar B-Q.

They built the light, woodsy building from scratch and plastered their customers' dollar bills all over one wall in the bar area. Watercolors by local artists add a pleasant color contrast, and the ambience is cozy and rustic, rather like what you'd expect Grandma's country place to be.

From its origin as a carry-out operation, the Buttonwood now does a healthy sit-down business. By trial and error they've found what works best in their recipes, sometimes changing the original ingredients. Black grouper, shark, and trout are a few of the seafood dishes available, and they're always fresh.

But the distinctive taste of their barbecue comes from buttonwood smoke. You'll read on the menu that *Conocarpus Erecta*, the buttonwood tree, is found on these islands in the transitional zones separating salt-water mangroves from fresh-water plants. Its flavor, when used for smoking fish, game, and other meat, is more delicate than that of hickory. The restaurant uses smaller pieces of the wood gleaned from thinning and trimming the trees rather than chopping down whole trees, as the size of these chips is more convenient.

Greg says they constantly strive for consistency in their cooking, which is one reason they've earned a good reputation. The cabbage for the cole slaw is hand cut, and you can tell that Diane especially loves to bake just by looking at the dessert tray full of the day's creations.

It's worth the trip out to the pass between Sanibel and Captiva.

Directions: The Buttonwood Bar B-Q is at 6410 Pine Road. You've shelled out your greenbacks for the toll over the Sanibel Causeway (SR 867), which is called Periwinkle Way through Sanibel. Follow 867 approximately 10 miles to the restaurant, just off the main road.

*While you're here: The twin islands of Sanibel and Captiva are unparalleled for exotic shelling, and visitors often return home with the stooping posture of beachcombers. Wildlife photographers and nature enthusiasts will have a field day at the peaceful **J.N. "Ding" Darling National Wildlife Refuge**, another unsurpassed natural resource.*

SMOKED MULLET

(Allow time to soak ahead)

fresh whole mullet
salt
pepper
garlic
paprika

Remove full fillet from each side of fish. Leave skin and scales on to act as a retainer for juices. Soak fillets approximately 2 hours in salt water. Remove and place on grill in smoker. Season with salt, pepper, garlic, and paprika to taste. Smoke with buttonwood mangrove*, if available, and cook until flaky, about 3 to 4 hours at 195°F.

Serves: 1–2
Preparation: 2 hours to soak
Cooking: 3 to 4 hours

"Don't leave Florida without trying it!"

*May substitute other

SMOKED MULLET SPREAD

2-3   fillets smoked mullet
½   C. chopped onion
½   C. chopped green pepper
½   C. chopped celery
2   8-oz. pkgs. cream cheese
¼-½   C. mayonnaise
       horseradish to taste
       paprika

Peel fish from skin and break into small pieces. Set aside. Add all ingredients to cream cheese and mix together to a smooth consistency. Add smoked mullet. Form into a ball and sprinkle with paprika. Refrigerate.

Serves: 6 as an hors d'oeuvre
Preparation: 10 minutes (allow time for chilling)

"Wonderful on crackers or as a spread for a sandwich!"

Buttonwood Bar B-Q
Sanibel

BUTTONWOOD CARROT CAKE

---

2   C. all-purpose flour
1½   C. sugar
2   T. baking soda
2   T. cinnamon
1   T. baking powder
½   T. salt
4   large eggs
1   C. mayonnaise (to make cake moist)
3   C. coarsely grated carrots, peeled
¾   C. pecans

Grease and flour an 8-cup bundt pan. Mix all dry ingredients together. Add eggs and mayonnaise and continue beating. Stir in carrots and pecans. Reserve 2 tablespoons of the batter to add to frosting. Pour remaining batter into bundt pan. Bake at 350°F. for 45-55 minutes or until a cake tester inserted into the middle comes out clean. Frost cake when cool with Cream Cheese Frosting on next page.

CREAM CHEESE FROSTING (makes about 2 cups)

2   3-oz. packages cream cheese at room temperature
2   T. reserved carrot cake batter
2   C. confectioners sugar, sifted if lumpy
1   T. vanilla extract

Beat cream cheese and batter in a medium-size bowl
at medium speed until no lumps remain. Add sugar
and vanilla. Beat at high speed until fluffy. Spread
over cake. You may have to add additional sugar to
get a spreadable consistency.

Yields: 1 cake
Preparation: 20–25 minutes
Cooking: 45–55 minutes

*"This is a rich cake that is not too spicy. If you
prefer one that is spicier, add more cinnamon and a
tablespoon of nutmeg."*

SEA TROUT OR GROUPER IN BEER BATTER

1   cup self-rising flour, plus extra for dipping
1   12-oz. can beer
1   T. baking powder
    pinch of salt and paprika
4-6 fish fillets

Combine 1 cup of flour and all other ingredients
except fish in a large bowl and mix well. Dip fish
fillets in flour, tap lightly with a knife so that the
flour adheres. Then dip fish in batter. Deep fry until
golden brown.

Serves: 4-6
Preparation: 2 minutes
Cooking: Depends upon thickness of fish

*"This is a light and delicious batter. Be sure not to
overcook the fish. We usually open the beer about an
hour before using, to get rid of some of the air
bubbles."*

The Crab Trap

Palmetto

It's a common sight on a summer evening to see pairs of kids or families ambling out by a pier or into a marshy area near brackish water. They'll be armed with dip-nets and cane poles, and hunks of fish or raw chicken as bait to catch a bucketful of blue crabs for dinner. Blue crab is one of some 4,500 species of crab worldwide and one that's especially popular in Florida.

Caught commercially, three shipments of blue crabs come in every week from Punta Gorda and are sent to The Crab Trap, where they end up in an assortment of winning dishes fixed as many ways as you can imagine. Owners Margaret and Lee Cline, formerly from the Chesapeake Bay area, have brought their Maryland recipes with them to adapt to what's caught locally. Lee has a penchant for things that are different, reflected in the European and Caribbean names applied to some of the entrees.

In addition to the variety of crab dishes, you'll find plenty of Florida regional fare ranging from 'gator and cooter to shark and swordfish, all depending on the season and availability. Even the side dishes are different—crab fritters, scalloped bananas, and clam-stuffed mushrooms. One of the tricks the Clines have learned is to use mayonnaise to baste the fish before broiling or frying so that the natural flavor is "sealed in."

Be prepared to wait for a seat. Lee's philosophy is to take the time required for each order to prepare it "exceptionally," rather than to rush through the cooking and end up with only mediocre results. You won't mind the wait, though, in the large and comfortable lounge area.

Take in the wall decor before you're seated at a table. Again, you'll notice the Clines' "different" touch. The lighting fixtures are original creations that Lee made out of fish traps. Cypress knees and cedar grace the walls, covered with woven grass and reeds. The hand-crafted exotic birds come from St. Croix. The cork on the booths isn't just for decorative purposes; it provides good acoustics as well.

Don't be surprised if you're asked for an opinion on a new dish the Clines may be trying out. On the other hand, don't by shy about suggesting a dish for them to test!

Directions: *The Crab Trap is located directly on U.S. 19 in Palmetto, north of Bradenton and Sarasota, two miles south of the south toll plaza of the Skyway Bridge into St. Petersburg.*

While you're here: *Just a few miles' hop across to U.S. 301 is the* **Judah P. Benjamin Confederate State Historic Site** *at* **Gamble Plantation.** *The mansion was built in the late 1840s by Major Robert Gamble, a successful officer during the Second Seminole War. For a time the plantation was the leading producer of sugar and molasses in Florida. It's fully restored with pre-Civil War furnishings. There are picnic facilities outdoors.*

CLAM-STUFFED MUSHROOMS

---

10 oz. fresh clams, cooked and minced
    about 3½ oz. liquor (brandy recommended)
1   C. Italian or plain bread crumbs
½   C. vermouth
½   C. butter or margarine, melted
    oregano to taste
½   C. finely chopped celery
¼ to ½ C. grated Romano cheese
    salt and pepper to taste
½   C. Parmesan cheese
12-18 large, fresh mushrooms, stems removed

Combine all ingredients except mushrooms. Stuff into mushrooms and bake at 400°F. for 10 to 15 minutes. Serve piping hot.

Serves: 4-6 as an hors d'oeuvre
Preparation: 5-10 minutes
Cooking: 10-15 minutes

"Before you add the oregano, be sure to crush it in the palms of your hands to release the flavor."

CRAB IMPERIAL

1½ lbs. back fin blue crab meat
3 T. butter
3 T. flour
1 C. milk
1 C. mayonnaise
1 T. Worcestershire
½ t. salt
⅛ t. Tabasco Sauce
1 egg, well beaten
paprika

Pick over crab meat for shells and cartilage. Set aside. Melt butter. Blend in flour. Cook, stirring constantly for a minute or two. Add milk and cook, stirring until thick. Blend in mayonnaise and seasonings. Fold in beaten egg. Then gently fold in the crab meat. Spoon into individual crab or scallop shells or casseroles. Sprinkle with paprika and bake at 400°F. for 10 to 12 minutes or until bubbly.

Serves: 6
Preparation: 10–15 minutes
Cooking: 15 minutes

"This dish is light and delicate. It's perfect as a first course or as a main dish. Add some parsley to garnish and serve with a tossed salad and bread sticks or hot garlic bread."

GLOSSARY

All-purpose flour — Plain flour that has no salt or baking powder added.

Blanch — To parboil for 30 to 60 seconds and then plunge in cold water.

Béchamel (see Cream Sauce)

Braise — To cook slowly in fat until brown, then adding a small amount of liquid, covering and simmering.

Brown sauce/Sauce Español — A rich beef stock reduced and thickened with roux. May be purchased as beef gravy.

Beurre manié — 1 t. flour mixed with 1 t. butter, for thickening soups and sauces. Shape into little balls and freeze to be used as needed.

Butterfly — To cut against the grain or cut lengthwise, leaving meat attached on one side. This is done for appearance and to tenderize.

Chop/Dice/Mince —

Chop = 1/4-inch cubes
Dice = 1/8-inch cubes
Mince = smallest cubes

Clarify/Clarified — To make butter clear by heating and removing all whey or sediment as it rises to the top. Then carefully strain. Clarified butter will keep for at least a week if tightly covered and refrigerated.

Crackermeal — Fine meal made from crackers, finer than cornmeal and used as a more delicate coating for meats. Can be purchased or made from unsalted soda crakers rolled on a wooden board with a rolling pan.

Cream sauce/Béchamel — White sauce made with milk.

1 T. butter
1 C. hot milk
1 T. flour
salt, pepper, nutmeg to taste

Make roux of butter and flour. Cook until smooth, about 2 minutes. Remove from heat. Slowly whisk in hot milk until smooth. Cook 1 minute more and season. (Yield: 1 cup)

Cream sauce is Béchamel made with cream instead of milk. Velouté is Béchamel made with white stock (such as chicken, veal, or fish) in place of milk.

Crêpes — Thin pancakes (use blender or food processor).

3–4 eggs
1 C. flour
1½ C. milk
½ tsp. salt
3 T. butter (melted)

Combine all ingredients in processor and blend until smooth. Allow batter to rest 1 hour before frying. May be kept in refrigerator for 1 week. Allow 2 T. for each crêpe in a 6-inch pan.

Deep-fry — To cook by immersing in hot oil or fat in a pan deep enough for oil to cover food completely.

De-glaze — To pour liquid such as wine, water, or stock in a cooking pan, scraping sides and bottom with a wooden spoon to loosen residue.

Demi-glaze — A reduced brown sauce.

Devein — To clean shrimp by removing black filament from the back, before or after cooking.

Dredge/Dust/Flour — To dip in or sprinkle lightly with flour.

Fatback — Pure pork fat that is cut from the back of the pig, fresh or salt-cured.

Fillet/Filet — To cut or slice fish that has been cleaned, deheaded, and scaled down both sides of the backbone. Boneless pieces of meat or fish are called fillets.

Fold — To mix one ingredient into another slowly and gently, without breaking, as with egg whites that must be kept light and fluffy.

Glaze — A thin, smooth coating such as milk, melted butter, or other ingredient brushed on top of food to give it a shiny appearance.

Grits — A favorite side dish for a Southern meal. They are broken grains from corn hominy, which is corn with the hull and germ removed.

Julienne — To cut into thin matchstick-like strips, or strips that are so cut.

Knead — To work a mass of dough into a uniform texture by folding and pressing with the heels of your hands until dough is smooth and elastic.

Marinate — To soak food in liquid usually pickled with vinegar or wine and oil as well as spices and herbs that both add flavor and tenderize the meat or fish. The liquid is called marinade.

Poach — To simmer gently in hot liquid, to cover.

Purée — To force food through a sieve or blend in food processor until smooth.

Reduce — To cook or simmer a liquid until it is less; to concentrate flavor.

Roux — An equal amount of butter and flour browned together until smooth. Used to thicken many sauces and gravies.

Salt Pork — Generally pork fat cured in salt.

Saute — To cook lightly in an open, shallow pan, with a small amount of butter or fat, browning evenly and sealing in the juices.

Score — To make shallow cuts in surface of meat.

Simmer — To cook in water or other liquid below or just at the boiling point.

Steam — To expose to water vapor by cooking with a small amount of boiling water in a tightly covered pan.

FLORIDA BEEF

Say "beef" and most people probably think of the Iowa corn-fed variety. But Florida has been raising cattle longer than any other state in the country. It all started when Ponce de Leon brought the first Andalusian cattle to the New World in the early 1500s.

These first scrub cows, forerunners of Texas Longhorns, were not very big. Some historians said they were "ridiculous" in appearance and not very good as beef or milk producers. But the cows were a hardy breed that could withstand Florida's climate and unexplored wilderness areas. Over the centuries, as breeding technology improved, Florida cattle improved to the extent that calves are now shipped to two-thirds of the United States, the greatest number being sent to the Texas Panhandle.

Florida is the only state in the Southeast classed as a range cattle state. While today's cattle are kept in large, fenced pastures, wild-looking cowboys in the old days used to herd the cows by cracking their whips as they rode. According to folklore, they were nicknamed "cracker cowboys," later shortened to just "cracker." Nowadays Cracker also means someone who was born and raised in Florida.

The largest producer of beef in the Southeast, Florida has recently concentrated on crossbreeding Brahmans with English or Continental breeds and other purebred stock. Restaurants serving steaks and chops are popular especially in the "heartland" area between Ocala, Lake Okeechobee, and the century-old cow town, Kissimmee. The cow camp at the Lake Kissimmee State Recreation Area, accessible from U.S. 27 near Lake Wales (call the recreation area for directions), is a colorful re-creation of what this aspect of Cracker life was like.

FRESH FLORIDA FRUITS AND CITRUS

Florida produces nearly 80 percent of all the oranges grown in the country and two-thirds of the country's total citrus crop. Half of the crop is frozen as juice concentrate, as juice, of course, is what the Florida orange is best known for. Some of the most popular varieties are Valencias (*the* juice orange), Tangelos (tangerine-grapefruit hybrids), Navels (good for eating), and Parson Browns (named for a 19th-century pastor who added to his insufficient income from preaching by growing oranges). Sour oranges, usually found growing wild, are used in many Spanish and Cuban recipes.

Grapefruit is not to be overlooked, either. Currently the Citrus Commission is testing both sugar-sweetened and low-calorie sweetened juices on the market. Kumquats and calamondins are close citrus relatives, favored for use in jellies and marmalade and as ornaments.

Florida grows mangoes which can be used at just about any stage of growth. This fruit originated in ancient India and spread to warm climates all over the world via trade routes of the explorers, reaching Florida just before the Civil War. Surprisingly, this luscious fruit is akin to poison ivy, and if you're allergic to its skin, you may want to wear gloves while handling it. Flavors range from a pineapple taste to peach to melon. A special treat is mango ice cream, which you can make very simply by blending one pint of diced ripe fruit with one quart of ice milk and freezing.

Papayas are melon-like fruits that can be used as vegetables when they are still green. This fruit also has a wide range of flavors and is often seasoned with lime juice and honey or sugar. One variety is sometimes called "pawpaw" in parts of the Caribbean.

Guavas are among the older fruits native to the American tropics, grown here even before European exploration. Yellow and strawberry guavas are the main types, and their variety of sweet flavors makes them delicious in jellies and pastries, or with squares of cream cheese.

Key Limes are Florida's best known tropical fruit, famous for their use in Key Lime pie. The pulp of these limes is yellow, not green. You can tell if the Key Lime pie you are being served is the real thing by its color. Enjoy!

'GATORS

There's quite a mystique about alligators, an unmistakably Florida symbol. The 18th-century botanist William Bartram wrote that they were so numerous in some parts of the state "that it would have been easy to have walked across on their heads had the animals been harmless."

Of course, they're *not* harmless. Those great snapping jaws can make mincemeat of a calf or even a fearsome Doberman, sending an unsuspecting victim to animal heaven in seconds. Over the decades, this descendant of dinosaurs has been valuable for its hide and its meat. Today the state has protected the species and is making an effort to manage its large, dynamic population and handle nuisance complaints.

At any given time, there are about 60 "alligator control agents" around the state. If there is a problem 'gator on your property, call the Florida Game and Fresh Water Fish Commission. When a complaint comes in, the agency issues a license for a trapper to capture the specific 'gator, either for relocation or for disposal. Generally, though, once a nuisance, always a nuisance, so disposal is more common. The trapper gets a percentage of sales for giving the hide to the state for auction, and he sells the meat to authorized restaurants.

You can't just go out and trap your own 'gator to make a meal of the beast. The days of poaching are pretty much gone, and it is illegal to trap one without a license. But a local folklore has sprung up that the hunter who was once known as the biggest poacher of all is now the operator of a hugely successful 'gator farm on Lake Okeechobee, one of only a handful of such farms in Florida.

The only legal way you may eat 'gator meat is cooked, and only restaurants are authorized to cook it. The most common way of serving 'gator is fried 'gator tail, in bite-sized pieces. The cooked meat is flavorful and white, like chicken, and sometimes can be chewy or tough, depending on the part of the 'gator that is used.

Better for *you* to bite the 'gator than the other way around!

SWAMP CABBAGE

Some people who don't like the thought of "roughing it" think they wouldn't like a dish with a name like swamp cabbage . . . until they learn that it's just the Cracker name for hearts of palm. Specifically, it's the heart of the sabal (cabbage) palm, Florida's state tree.

Actually, this "tree" is botanically a "monocot." That's short for monocotyledon, plants whose embryos produce single parallel-veined leaves. Once the bud is destroyed, the plant dies. Thus, this kind of "tree" is really more like a lily than a real tree that produces not one but two such leaves so that it can proliferate.

Marjorie Kinnan Rawlings had voiced the concern of many back-country folk when she wrote *Cross Creek Cookery*, saying ". . . this greatest of Florida vegetables is the white core of a young palm tree, and its cutting means the death of the tree." Fearing that the groves might eventually be wiped out, she pointed out a better reason for the tree's value, as an anchor to identify the location of a sportsman's camp. She did acknowledge, though, that bears knew the food value of swamp cabbage. The best trees are those that are eight to 10 feet tall, growing not too close to the water, she wrote.

Today the sabal palm is protected by state law. A permit is required from the Florida Department of Agriculture and Consumer Services for removal and harvesting. But while the fresh plant is available only under certain circumstances, the canned version in the gourmet sections of grocery stores is readily available for modern cooks who prefer convenience. And not only is the plant good for food, but its fiber, used to make brushes and brooms worldwide, is the only natural brush fiber grown and processed in the country.

Swamp cabbage mixes so well with other foods that you can even make a main course of it. Actually, it's *better* when prepared with another flavoring, as it can taste bland, even bitter, when served alone. The Seminole Indians add canned syrup and salt, for example. Salt pork, any cured pork cut (ham hock, smoked bacon, pork shoulder, and so forth) and most wild game all make good seasonings.

Experiment with the recipes we've provided and some of your own, and you'll see how easily swamp cabbage can become part of your everyday menu.

CONCH

Key lime pie may be the most famous individual dish from the Florida Keys, but "conch is king" as a staple. The rose-pink spiral shellfish contains a sweet-flavored, juicy meat that lends itself to a variety of recipes.

The conch is so much a part of Keys menus that its name is also the nickname of native residents. Historically, a *real* conch (say KONK) is a descendant of one of the original Bahamian renegade families who came in search of turtles and wood for building. Defiantly independent, they swore they'd "eat conch" before they'd pay high British taxes. And eat conch they did, liked it, and the name stuck. Conch cuisine today is a curious mixture of cockney, tangy Caribbean, Cracker, and Latin-American influences.

The largest species found in North America, the Florida conch is housed in an attractive shell often used for decoration and as a horn. There's more to removing the animal inside than just breaking the tip of the shell and inserting a fine, thin knife blade to cut the snail away from the muscle that holds it in place. It takes practice, but once you're experienced, you should be able to do it very quickly.

Other ways of removing the meat in order to preserve the shell are to boil it or apply heat to the tip, or to entice the snail out by rubbing its exposed area with salt, grabbing and pulling hard.

The meat is tough and needs to be marinated first, beaten with a mallet, or cooked at length to tenderize it. Conch is good raw, too, in a salad or eaten like oysters, but Key lime juice will help soften the meat first. Try it the way the natives prepare it, by making "old sour." Dissolve one tablespoon of salt in a pint of lime juice, ferment at room temperature at least two weeks, and then marinate the conch. Add a dash of cayenne pepper if you want an extra hot zing.

284

MINORCAN SPECIALTIES

Some of Florida's most distinctive ethnic foods have been kept alive in St. Augustine's Minorcan community. Led by Dr. Andrew Turnbull, a group of settlers from the Mediterranean island of Minorca had come to New Smyrna Beach in the 1700s. But with dwindling food supplies and the ravages of illness, the colony ended in 1777, and those who could fled to the north.

Three significant Minorcan foods are datil peppers (say DATtle), pilau (say PERlo in the northern part of the state, PEElow everywhere else in the state), and Fromajardis pastries (say FROmaZHARdis).

The Minorcan colonists brought datil peppers with them from the Mediterranean as a mainstay of the culture's cooking. The small, green-orange plants appear harmless but have been called "bottled hell" by the uninitiated who charge into datil pepper jelly and datil pepper relish. No Minorcan stock bases are complete without this seasoning. "Heavenly torture," as it is also called, is so necessary to Minorcan recipes and grown by many area cooks in their own backyards. It's impossible to imagine any restaurant in town that doesn't use this seasoning in its recipes.

Pilau begins with a seasoned rice base. Chicken or shrimp pilau are among several common varieties, but there have been times when, if a certain kind of meat was not available, the dish would be prepared with speckled butter beans instead. Start by making a thick "mulch" paste by cooking down datil peppers, onions, tomatoes, green peppers, and other seasonings in a cast-iron pot until the mixture is dark in color, almost burnt. Then add your choice of meat, rice and water. Simmer. The more "seasoned" the iron pot is, the better the flavor. You can "cure" a new skillet with oil and vegetable trimmings by cooking until food no longer sticks or turns black.

Fromajardis pastries are stuffed with cheese and baked for Easter Eve festival celebrations. In the 1770s, young men would go caroling from house to house, praising homeowners who served them the cakes and condemning those who didn't. Today the cakes are considered a traditional Minorcan breakfast.

The original New Smyrna settlement may not have survived, but thanks to the spirit of self-sufficiency among generations of Minorcans, their customs remain.

WHERE TO GET ANSWERS ABOUT FLORIDA'S PLANT AND ANIMAL LIFE

What's okay to eat . . . What isn't

A number of the recipes in FAMOUS FLORIDA! CRACKER COOKIN' AND OTHER FAVORITES call for ingredients that are protected by state law. That means you may not necessarily be able to prepare some of them yourself, such as alligator, but you can certainly enjoy them in the restaurants they're served in. You'll be the wiser for knowing how to fix them.

Certain other native ingredients are available to you, but you will need to be aware of laws and restrictions that may apply regarding season dates and allowable quantities. The following state agencies will gladly answer your questions and send helpful material for your own reference.

Department of Natural Resources
(also has information on state parks, recreation, and camping facilities)
Crown Building, Room 620
202 Blount Street
Tallahassee, FL 32301

Department of Agriculture and Consumer Services
The Capitol
Tallahassee, FL 32301

Game and Fresh Water Fish Commission
Farris Bryant Building
620 S. Meridien Street
Tallahassee, FL 32301

School of Forest Resources and Conservation
University of Florida
Gainesville, FL 32611

The **University of Miami Marine Lab** and **Sea World** in Orlando are two other important educational resources for information on all forms of marine life.

FLORIDA FESTIVALS—CRACKER, PIONEER, FOOD SPECIALTIES, SEAFOOD, FAIRS

This is a selected listing of events that you'll enjoy for their focus on Florida regional foods and historic traditions. For details, contact the Chamber of Commerce in the named communities. Be sure to check if the activity hasn't been rescheduled to a different month.

January

Collier County Fair, Naples
South Florida Fair, West Palm Beach
Manatee County Fair, Palmetto
Southwest Florida Fair, Fort Myers
Silver Sailfish Derby of the Palm Beaches, West Palm Beach
Annual Homestead Rodeo, Homestead

February

Florida State Fair, Tampa
Highlands County Fair, Sebring
Florida Citrus Festival, Winter Haven
South Dade County Fair, Homestead
Southeastern Youth Fair, Ocala
St. Lucie County Fair, Fort Pierce
Pasco County Fair, Dade City
Hendry County Fair, Clewiston
Kissimmee Valley Fair and Livestock Show, Kissimmee
DeSoto County Fair, Arcadia
Central Florida Fair, Orlando
Hillsborough County Fair and Strawberry Festival, Plant City
Everglades City Fishermen's Seafood Festival
Seminole Tribal Fair, Hollywood
Grant Seafood Festival, Grant (Melbourne)
Heart of Florida Folk Festival, Dade City
Swamp Cabbage Festival, LaBelle
Silver Spurs Rodeo, Kissimmee

March

Citrus County Fair, Inverness
Martin County Fair, Stuart
Pinellas County Fair, Largo
Sarasota County Fair, Sarasota
Lake County Fair and Flower Show, Eustis
Suwannee River Fair and Livestock Show, Suwannee County, Chiefland
Dade County Youth Fair, Miami
Polk County Youth Fair, Bartow
Baker County Fair, MacClenny
Hernando County Fair, Brooksville
Putnam County Fair, Palatka
Pioneer Park Days, Zolfo Springs
Orange Blossom Festival, Davie
Chalo Nitka (Bass) Festival and Rodeo, Moore Haven
Seafood Festival, Marathon
Winter Harvest, Goulds
Carnaval Miami, Little Havana, Miami
Annual Bonita Springs Festival (Tomato-Snook Festival), Bonita Springs
Speckled Perch Festival, Okeechobee
Withlacoochee Backwater Jamboree, Dunnellon
Flagler County Cracker Day, Bunnell
All-Florida Championship Rodeo, Arcadia

April

Bradford County Fair, Starke
St. Johns River Catfish Festival, Crescent City
Largo Cracker Supper, Largo
Bounty of the Sea Seafood Festival, Miami
Black Gold Jubilee (Everglades harvest), Belle Glade
State Beef Cook-Off, Naples
Indian River Festival, Titusville
Down Home Days, DeLand
District Rodeo, Palatka
Island Open Fishing Derby, Sanibel Island

May

Boom Town Days, Dunnellon
Florida Folk Festival, White Springs

Zellwood Sweet Corn Festival, Zellwood
Annual Fishing Tournament, St. Augustine
Summer Fishing Contest, West Palm Beach
Summer Fishing Tournament, Pompano Beach
Rodeo Week, Jasper
Pompano Beach Fishing Rodeo, Pompano Beach
Marathon Dolphin Scramble, Marathon
Greater Daytona Beach Area Striking Fish Tournament,
    Daytona Beach

June

Sea Turtle Watch, Jensen Beach
Cross and Sword (state play), St. Augustine
Panhandle Watermelon Festival, Chipley
Jefferson County Watermelon Festival, Monticello
Chiefland Watermelon Festival, Chiefland
Charlotte Harbor Fishing Tournament, Port Charlotte
International Bonefish Tournament, Marathon
Pensacola Shark Rodeo, Pensacola

July

Everglades Outdoor Music Festival, Miami
All-Florida Championship Rodeo, Arcadia
Silver Spurs Rodeo, Kissimmee
Destin Shark Tournament, Destin
Marathon Jaycees Shark Tournament, Marathon
Greater Jacksonville King Mackerel Tournament,
    Jacksonville

August

Wausau Fun Day and Possum Festival, Wausau
Fort Walton Beach/Destin Open Billfish Tournament,
    Fort Walton Beach
Pensacola Ladies' Billfish Tournament, Pensacola
Captain's Billfishing Tournament, Panama City Beach
Gulf Coast Masters Invitational Billfish Tournament,
    Pensacola
Annual Fishathon, St. Petersburg

September

International Worm Fiddling Contest, Carywille
Panacea Blue Crab Festival, Panacea
Pioneer Days, Englewood
Pioneer Florida Festival, Dade City
Seafood Festival, Pensacola
Creek Indian Pow-Wow, Pensacola
Bellview Junction Western Round-Up, Pensacola
Offshore Sportfishing Tournament, Sebastian Inlet
Cattlemen's Labor Day Rodeo, Okeechobee
Open Spearfishing Tournament, Panama City
Marlborough Billfishing Tournament, Destin
Miracle Strip King Mackerel Tournament, Panama City

October

Northeast Florida Fair, Callahan
Pensacola Interstate Fair, Pensacola
Greater Jacksonville Fair, Jacksonville
Suwannee County Fair, Live Oak
Jackson County Fair, Marianna
Greater Holmes County Fair, Bonifay
Bay County Fair, Panama City
Okaloosa County Fair, Fort Walton Beach
North Florida Fair, Tallahassee
Country Jubilee, Largo
World's Chicken Pluckin' Championship, Spring Hill
Destin Seafood Festival, Destin
Oak Hill Seafood Festival, Oak Hill
Cracker Day, St. Augustine
Florida Forest Festival, Perry
Rattlesnake Festival/International Gopher Race,
    San Antonio
Seafood Festival, Cedar Key
Boggy Bayou Mullet Festival, Niceville
Brighton Field Days, Brighton Seminole Reservation
Pioneer Days Folk Festival, Orlando
Czechoslovakian Independence Day, Masaryktown
Hispanic Heritage Festival, Dade County, Miami
Jeanie Auditions and Ball, White Springs
Destin October Fishing Rodeo, Destin
Swamp Buggy Races, Naples
Seafood Festival, Panama City Beach

November

Columbia County Fair, Lake City
Alachua County Fair, Gainesville
Volusia County Fair and Youth Show, DeLand
Broward County Fair, Hollywood
Florida Seafood Festival, Apalachicola
Seafood Festival, Madeira Beach
The Harvest, Miami
Winter Fishing Contest, West Palm Beach
Winter Fishing Tournament, Pompano Beach
Championship Rodeo, Davie

December

December on the Farm, Tallahassee
Miccosukee Tribe's Annual Indian Art Festival, Miami
Stuart Sailfish Club Light Tackle Tournament, Stuart
Fishing Bowl, West Palm Beach

—NOTES—

REFERENCES

If you'd like to delve deeper into Florida's traditional foodways, history, and places where you can find these dishes, the following list of books and pamphlets will be helpful. Some of the titles may be out of print, but your local public library or university library may have them or may be able to arrange an inter-library loan. Many are still available at bookstores and gift shops. We've listed them alphabetically by title, for your convenience, with available information about the publisher. Titles shown in **BOLDFACE CAPITAL LETTERS** are the ones we feel are of greatest interest.

American Cooking: Southern Style (1968), by Eugene Walter. Time-Life Books, New York. Florida's specialties in this volume include hearts of palm, fruits and shellfish. 208 pp., hardcover.

Apalachicola Seafood Recipes, by Mr. Sherlock. Printed by Valley Litho, Old Town, FL. 55 pp., paper.

Aunt Nancy's Suwannee Country Cooking (1971), by Nancy Morgan. White Springs, FL. 32 pp., paper.

Bay Leaves (1975), by the Junior Service League of Panama City Inc., Panama City, FL. Notes on early days, traditional and contemporary recipes. 352 pp., spiral.

The Beach Cookbook (1976), by Jane Hodges Hamm. Strode Publishers Inc., Huntsville, AL. Recipes from the Gulf of Mexico, Atlantic and Pacific coasts, all in one collection. 236 pp., paper.

Citrus Cooking (1972), by Beatrice Vaughan. Stephen Greene Press, Brattleboro, VT. This Harvest Home cookbook is by a winter resident of Mt. Dora, FL. 32 pp., paper.

CLARITA'S COCINA (1970), by Clarita Garcia. Doubleday, New York. "Great traditional recipes from a Spanish kitchen." 384 pp., hardcover.

Conch Cooking. Florida Keys Printing and Publishing, Key West. English and Cuban methods of preparing foods, with informative notes about each dish. 93 pp., paper.

Cross Creek (original copyright 1942; still in print), by Marjorie Kinnan Rawlings. Mockingbird Books Inc., St. Simons Island, GA. The Pulitzer-Prize-winning author's narrative of life in this tiny, backwoods town. The chapter "Our daily bread" vividly describes their foodways. 279 pp., paper.

CROSS CREEK COOKERY (1942), by Marjorie Kinnan Rawlings. Charles Scribner's Sons, New York. Illustrated by Robert Camp, Jr. Written in the author's inimitable conversational narrative, just as if she were telling you in person how each dish is prepared. Menus, too. 230 pp., paper.

CROSS CREEK KITCHENS, by Sally Morrisson. Triad Publishing Company, Gainesville, FL. The author is curator at the Marjorie Kinnan Rawlings State Historic Site. Recipes and narrative.

Cypress Gardens Cookbook (1970), by the St. Agnes Welfare Guild, St. Paul's Episcopal Church. Winter Haven, FL. Starts out, even before the title page, with the Florida Citrus Commission's Waverly grapefruit diet. Many local food recipes. 330 pp., paper.

Dock to Dish/What To Do with a Fish: Florida Seafood Secrets (1981), by Eat More Fish Inc. Distributed by F & F Sales, Miami, FL. Hints on keeping and dressing fish, preparation, and recipes, presented simply and lightheartedly. 34 pp., paper.

EATING IN AMERICA: A HISTORY (1976), by Waverley Root and Richard de Rochemont. William Morrow and Company Inc., New York. Praised and panned by the critics, this is one of the most comprehensive narratives about food, both simple and gourmet, eaten in the United States. Includes a partially annotated bibliography. 512 pp., hardcover.

Eat Well in Key West (1982), by Dan McDonald. De Gustibus Guides of Florida Inc., Key West, FL. Independent restaurant reviews by a former New York City restaurant manager and travel escort for American Express. 36 pp., paper.

1890 Festival Cookbook (1975), edited by Sadie Coram Alston. Friends of McIntosh Inc., McIntosh, FL. Country recipes from the McIntosh area (Marion County). 134 pp., paper.

FLORIDA RECIPES: 300 YEARS OF GOOD EATING (1972), by Lowis Carlton. Each chapter of regional recipes is preceded by an informative narrative of the history of that part of the state and its favorite foods. 80 pp., paper.

FAMOUS FLORIDA!™ RESTAURANTS & RECIPES (1981), by Sandi Brown and Joyce LaFray-Young. Specialty dishes of 50 of Florida's top restaurants, with restaurant reviews, recipes, and suggestions for day trips. 320 pp., paper.

FAMOUS FLORIDA!™ UNDERGROUND GOURMET (1981), by Barbie Baldwin. Gourmet and down-home recipes from off-the-beaten-path restaurants. 320 pp., paper.

FAMOUS FLORIDA! THE UNDERWATER GOURMET (1983), by Joyce LaFray-Young, Susan Shepard and Laura De Salvo. Recipes from 90 of Florida's best seafood restaurants, with tips on preparation and buying fresh seafood. 320 pp., paper.

THE FLORIDA BICENTENNIAL TRAIL: A HERITAGE REVISITED (1976), by the Bicentennial Commission of Florida in cooperation with the Florida Department of Commerce. Historical sketches of both famous and lesser-known landmarks, state museums and historic towns, with a pull-out map locating each site along the trail. 134 pp., paper.

FLORIDA COWMAN: A HISTORY OF FLORIDA CATTLE RAISING (1976), by Joe A. Akerman, Jr. Florida Cattleman's Association, Kissimmee, FL. Lots of solid history, interviews with old-timers, and anecdotes. Illustrated. Extensive bibliography. 286 pp., hardcover.

FLORIDA FOLK FESTIVAL SOUVENIR PROGRAMS (1980–1983). Florida Folk Life Program, White Springs, FL. In addition to the performance schedule, includes interesting and informative notes by professional folklorists on foodways from selected regions featured each year. Paper.

THE FLORIDA HERITAGE COOKBOOK/BICENTENNIAL EDITION (1976), by Marina Polvay and Marilyn Fellman. Florida Consultation and Management Inc., Miami, FL. Presents the state's "rich and fascinating food heritage" with readable historical narrative at the beginning of each chapter. Glossary of fish, fruit and vegetables, with several color photos. 160 pp., paper.

Florida Keys Cooking (1980), by Patricia Artman. Key West, FL. Recipes. 24 pp., paper.

Florida Seafood: Basics and Beyond, by the Division of Marine Resources, Department of Natural Resources, Harmon Shields, Executive Director. How to clean fish, different cooking methods, notes, and recipes for selected Florida species. 32 pp., paper.

Florida's Favorite Seafoods (1960), by the Florida Board of Conservation, Randolph Hodges, Director. Peninsular Publishing Company, Tallahassee, FL. 63 pp., paper.

Florida's Good Eating: Typical Cooking with a Touch of History (1978), by Blanche Mercer Fearington. DeLand, FL. Illustrations of historic sites by Evie Salter. Some recipes have historic introductions. 252 pp., paper.

FLORIDA'S VANISHING WILDLIFE (1982), by Laurel Comella Hendry, Thomas M. Goodwin, and Ronald F. Labisky. Florida Cooperative Extension Service in cooperation with other agencies, University of Florida, Gainesville, FL. Summaries of the protected status of 29 species of wildlife as of 1982; their life history, habitat and distribution, reasons for decline, and protective measures. 69 pp., paper.

Food Favorites of St. Augustine (1973), by Joan Adams Wickham. C.F. Hamblen Inc., St. Augustine, FL. Spanish, Minorcan, English, and American recipes, presented in a format based on Jean Gordon's 1958 Rose Recipes: Customs, Facts and Fancies. Chronology of dates and some of the most readable historical notes precede recipes. 188 pp., hardcover.

THE GASPARILLA COOKBOOK (1961), by the Junior League of Tampa. Tampa, FL. Illustrations by Lamar Sparkman. 326 pp., hardcover.

GOODFOOD: THE ADVENTUROUS EATER'S GUIDE TO RESTAURANTS SERVING AMERICA'S BEST REGIONAL SPECIALTIES (1983), by Jane and Michael Stern. Alfred A. Knopf Inc., New York. Written by the authors of **Roadfood**, a "survival guide for highway travelers." The Sterns have been popularizing their discoveries on National Public Radio's program, "All Things Considered." The character of regional cooking, as found in the nation's restaurants, is presented by region, with maps, organized into categories by type of restaurant and type of specialty, starring the authors' top picks. 460 pp., paper.

How to Smoke Seafood, Florida Cracker Style (1971), by Ted Dahlen. Types of smokers, preparing fish, types of wood, how much heat, flavoring/seasoning/smoking, recipes.

JANE NICKERSON'S FLORIDA COOKBOOK (1973), by Jane Nickerson. University of Florida Press, Gainesville, FL. As the introduction states, "Florida is a good cook's dream come true, where anyone fascinated with the kitchen art can find an abundance of ingredients without going to market." Includes a list of lesser known Florida fruits and vegetables. 204 pp., hardcover.

Louise Lamme's Florida Cook Book (1968), by Louise Lamme. Star Press, Boynton Beach, FL. Both "Old Timey" and modern Florida dishes, including Seminole Indian recipes and fresh rattlesnake recipes. Narrative describes recipes and history. 68 pp., paper.

Louise Lamme's Florida Seafood Cook Book (1973), by Louise Lamme. Star Publishing Company, Boynton Beach, FL. How to prepare seafood recipes and appropriate side dishes such as hushpuppies and grits. 48 pp., paper.

Old Customs of Pensacola and Favorite Recipes of the Times (1974). Historic Pensacola Preservation Society, Pensacola, FL. An outline of the city's best-loved folklore. Paper.

Oranges (1967), by John McPhee. Farrar, Straus & Giroux, New York. Articles that originally appeared in *The New Yorker* magazine. 149 pp., hardcover.

PALM BEACH ENTERTAINS (1976), by the Junior League of the Palm Beaches Inc. Coward, McCann & Geoghegan Inc. Part I is a 68–page history of Palm Beach, as entertaining as the recipes that follow. 241 pp., hardcover.

THE PIONEER COOK IN SOUTHEAST FLORIDA (1975), by Donald Walter Curl. Boca Raton Historical Society, Boca Raton, FL. With archive-style pen and ink etchings. This is a must-read social history, with historic recipes, descriptions of fruits found in southeast Florida yards today, and contemporary recipes. 70 pp., paper.

St. Augustine Cookery (1965), by the Flagler Hospital Auxiliary. Flagler Hospital, St. Augustine, FL. Recipes handed down by Spanish, French, English and American settlers. 20 pp., paper.

Seafood Adventures from the Gulf and South Atlantic, by the Gulf and South Atlantic Fisheries Development Foundation Inc., Tampa, FL. Nutritional features, purchasing, cleaning and dressing, basic and special cooking methods, storage of seafood. Short description of selected fish, with recipes. 72 pp., paper.

South Florida Cookery: Unique Recipes from the Tropics and Elsewhere (1964), by Alex D. Hawkes. Wake Brooks House, Coral Gables, FL. 224 pp., handmade hardcover.

Spanish and Minorcan Recipes from Historic Old St. Augustine (1940s), by Mary Lee Cannon. Includes thumbnail history of North Aviles Street by K.S. Lawson, and story of the Minorcans, by E.W. Lawson.

THE TRAVELS OF WILLIAM BARTRAM (originally published in 1791; 1980 reprint), by William Bartram. Latest printing available from Peregrine Smith, Layton, UT. One of the earliest starting points for Florida's recorded history in the English language. Written by a botanist in an eloquent style that has almost disappeared today. The portrait of life and cuisine in those times would be incomparable were it not for the images that Samuel Coleridge Taylor drew from for several of his epic poems. 332 pages, paper.

—NOTES—

INDEX

296

Desserts

298

Back on Those Back Roads Again

Last summer (1982) I drove 7,000 miles across America to find out if it's still there, and in case you're interested, it is.

Chorus:

> Well I'm travelin' down the back roads, not goin' anywhere,
> Wavin' at the country folks on the front porch in their chair,
> That little boy with the fishin' pole don't know that I'd exchange
> Everything I've got right now to be him once again.

When I left New York City, went on that interstate,
That long wide ribbon of concrete was more than I could take.
So when I hit Virginia, I found a country lane,
And I got back on those back roads again.

From the hills of North Carolina to Georgia's bottom land
I never drove on one paved road or went through one big town.
Just red clay banks and country shacks and a swimming hole now
  and then
'Cause I'm back on those back roads again.

Went from Georgia down to Florida 'cause the road that I was on
Didn't know where I was goin', wouldn't have cared if it had known.
You can keep your crowded cities, just give me the land
And put me on those back roads again.

I said I'm travelin' down the back roads, not goin' anywhere,
Wavin' at the country folks on the front porch in their chair,
That little boy with the fishin' pole don't know that I'd exchange
Everything I've got right now to be him once again.
Set me down on a river bank; put a cane pole in my hand,
I'm back on those back roads again.
I said I'm back on those back roads again.

(Don Grooms is a professor of broadcasting at the University of Florida in Gainesville. A Cherokee Indian, he is a regular entertainer at the annual Florida Folk Festival.)

—NOTES—

ORDER FORM

Send LaFRAY PUBLISHING COMPANY
to: P. O. Box 76400, St. Petersburg, FL 33734
Phone: (813) 821-3233

_____ copies of *Cracker Cookin' ™ and Other* $ _____
Favorites @ $9.95 each
_____ copies of *The Underwater Gourmet™* $ _____
The Great Seafood Book @ $9.95 each
_____ copies of *Famous Florida!™* $ _____
Restaurants & Recipes @ $9.95 each
Add postage and handling @ $2.00 each $ _____
Florida residents add 5% sales tax @ $ _____
$.50 each

TOTAL ENCLOSED $ _____

Send LaFRAY PUBLISHING COMPANY
to: P. O. Box 76400, St. Petersburg, FL 33734
Phone: (813) 821-3233

_____ copies of *Cracker Cookin' ™ and Other* $ _____
Favorites @ $9.95 each
_____ copies of *The Underwater Gourmet™* $ _____
The Great Seafood Book @ $9.95 each
_____ copies of *Famous Florida!™* $ _____
Restaurants & Recipes @ $9.95 each
Add postage and handling @ $2.00 each $ _____
Florida residents add 5% sales tax @ $ _____
$.50 each

TOTAL ENCLOSED $ _____

Send LaFRAY PUBLISHING COMPANY
to: P. O. Box 76400, St. Petersburg, FL 33734
Phone: (813) 821-3233

_____ copies of *Cracker Cookin' ™ and Other* $ _____
Favorites @ $9.95 each
_____ copies of *The Underwater Gourmet™* $ _____
The Great Seafood Book @ $9.95 each
_____ copies of *Famous Florida!™* $ _____
Restaurants & Recipes @ $9.95 each
Add postage and handling @ $2.00 each $ _____
Florida residents add 5% sales tax @ $ _____
$.50 each

TOTAL ENCLOSED $ _____
